Praise for *Sex ...*

Skye Alexander's *Sex Magic for Beginners* is a great introduction for people who want to learn the concepts of harnessing the incredible energies raised during sex and putting them to magical use. Wonderfully specific and positively fun, it is serious about the subject without being tedious or dry. It also allows people from all backgrounds to use sex magick to enhance virtually any form of magick they're currently using, including talismans, sigils, crystals, candles, and several other systems.

—Donald Michael Kraig
Author of *Modern Sex Magick*

Sex Magic
For Beginners

About the Author

Skye Alexander is the author of more than thirty fiction and nonfiction books. Her stories and essays have appeared in numerous anthologies internationally, and her work has been translated into ten languages. The Discovery Channel TV special *Secret Stonehenge* featured her doing a ritual at Stonehenge. After spending thirty-one years in Massachusetts, she now lives in Texas with her familiar, Domino. She invites you to visit her website and blog: www.skyealexander.com.

To Write to the Author

If you wish to contact the author or would like more information about this book, please write to the author in care of Llewellyn Worldwide, and we will forward your request. Both the author and publisher appreciate hearing from you and learning of your enjoyment of this book and how it has helped you. Llewellyn Worldwide cannot guarantee that every letter written to the author can be answered, but all will be forwarded. Please write to:

Skye Alexander
℅ Llewellyn Worldwide
2143 Wooddale Drive
Woodbury, MN 55125-2989

Please enclose a self-addressed stamped envelope for reply,
or $1.00 to cover costs. If outside the USA, enclose
an international postal reply coupon.

Sex Magic

For Beginners

The Easy & Fun Way to Tap
into the Law of Attraction

SKYE ALEXANDER

Llewellyn Publications
Woodbury, Minnesota

FIRST EDITION
Sixth Printing, 2018

Book format by Bob Gaul
Cover art © plainpicture/beyond
Cover design by Adrienne Zimiga
Editing by Ed Day
Interior art © Llewellyn art department

Llewellyn Publications is a registered trademark of Llewellyn Worldwide Ltd.

Library of Congress Cataloging-in-Publication Data
Alexander, Skye.
 Sex magic for beginners: the easy and fun way to tap into the law of attraction / Skye Alexander.
    p. cm.
 Includes bibliographical references and index.
 ISBN 978-0-7387-2637-3
1. Magic. 2. Sex—Miscellanea. 3. Sexual attraction. I. Title.
 BF1623.S4A44 2011
 133.4'3—dc23
                        2011025106

Llewellyn Publications
A Division of Llewellyn Worldwide Ltd.
2143 Wooddale Drive
Woodbury, MN 55125-2989
www.llewellyn.com

Printed in the United States of America

Dedication

To all the men I've loved,
past and present,
and to those who will enrich
my life in the future.

Acknowledgments

No book is a singular effort and I wish to thank the many people who helped make this one a reality, including Holly Schmidt of Ravenous Romance/Hollan Publishing for her agenting expertise, Carrie Obry and Elysia Gallo for their encouragement and editorial savvy, and the rest of the staff at Llewellyn. I am also indebted to all the magicians past and present whose knowledge has informed mine, especially Rob Peregrine and Don Kraig, and to R. L., who launched me on this journey. Most of all, I'm grateful to Ron Conroy for providing a safe haven for me while I wrote this book.

contents

two: Consciously Creating Circumstances in Your Life / 17

three: Putting Sex Magic in Perspective / 29

eight: Empowering
Your Intentions / 131

introduction

Nobody knows exactly when or where sex magic originated. Some sources say it dates back to Adam and
his first wife, Lilith (Eve's predecessor), who according to
Hebrew mythology had an independent streak and liked
to be on top during sex. Others point to the fertility rites
of Europe's pre-Christian peoples and their sex-based celebrations, such as Beltane. Then there's Tantra, the mystical path of ecstasy whose rituals glorify sex, which began
some 6,000 years ago in India. And let's not overlook the
practices of the ancient Egyptians, Babylonians, Greeks,
Romans, Persians, Chinese, Maya—and perhaps a whole lot
of other folks who didn't bother to record their intimate
activities for posterity.

Much of the sex magic that's been handed down to us modern Westerners derives from two very different traditions: the Old World Northern European/Celtic/British Isles earth-centered cultures, and the Middle Eastern/Egyptian/Hebrew/Kabbalistic schools of thought. The latter, fostered by noted and notorious occult societies during the nineteenth and early twentieth centuries, is more complex in its ideology, rituals, and symbology. The former, which Neopagans and Wiccans often embrace, is more user-friendly and less cerebral. Tantra also has its followers in the West, and expresses yet another set of perspectives and practices that are rooted in Hindu spirituality. As you might suspect, different factions disagree in as many areas as they agree.

For our purposes here, sex magic's religious and/or ethnic roots, as well as the personalities connected with the various systems, are less relevant than its practical applications and its potential for us today. My objective is to explain the basics: what, why, when, and how. Think of this as a do-it-yourself primer of sex magic, not a comprehensive treatise.

Naturally, much information will necessarily be omitted due to space constraints. In the Resources section at the end of this book, I've recommended places to turn to for additional material. What I've chosen to present are certain ideas and techniques that I've found useful and pleasurable. Virtually anyone with the inclination and some determination can successfully utilize these practices to create the life circumstances you desire. Combine them with other types of magic, if you like. Explore, experiment, and enjoy.

In case you're wondering, this book isn't about how to revive the magic in your love life—although that certainly can happen. Nor is it a sex manual to help you get more satisfaction from your intimate experiences—although that can certainly happen as well. It's a nuts-and-bolts guide to using sexual energy to attract anything you want.

Sexual energy is natural, readily accessible, and incredibly powerful. It's your birthright, a key to health, wealth, and happiness—literally at your fingertips. For centuries, the secrets of sex magic have been shrouded in mystery. Now they're being revealed for all who wish to claim and make use of this knowledge. I firmly believe that anyone who chooses to go down this path will be richly rewarded.

I don't intend to moralize, euphonize, or patronize in this book—I'm not your mama—although from time to time I might raise questions for you to consider or point out potential dilemmas. It's up to you how you use the information. My observations have shown me that people only learn through experience. Therefore, I urge you to "just do it."

one

The Secret
of Sex Magic

What would you think if I said you can have everything you want? What if I said you already have everything you think? Once you understand that both are true, you're on your way to becoming a magician.

Now, what if I told you that you don't need to work long and hard in order to attract the good things in life? Money, success, love—anything you choose—are yours for the asking. All you have to do is make mad, passionate love as often as possible. That may sound too good to be true, but magicians around the world have known this secret for thousands of years, and they've used their sexual energy to reap all sorts of benefits. You can, too.

Most people want to lead better lives. We want to be happier, healthier, wealthier, or whatever. We'd like to take control of what happens to us instead of being at the mercy of chance, fate, or other people's agendas. That's why most magicians do spells in the first place. Magic enables you to harness the raw energy in the universe and direct it to produce the outcomes you choose. Magic lets you attract what you desire in life and protect yourself from pitfalls. Although you can do this with any type of magic, sex magic is an especially effective way to accomplish your objectives.

Maybe you're saying to yourself, *My sex life is pretty good. But I'm still in debt and struggling to make ends meet. What's the deal?* The simple answer is you're not doing it right. No, I'm not talking about what goes where. I'm sure you know how to fit tab A into slot B. What I mean is you think sex is just something that feels good and makes babies—and that mindset is limiting your possibilities. You don't realize sex has much more to offer you. You haven't yet learned to mobilize this powerful attracting force that abides within you and utilize it to shape your world. Well, all that is about to change.

What Is Sex Magic Anyway?

First, let me explain what sex magic *isn't*. Sex magic isn't some sort of kinky parlor game. It's not intended to jazz up a lackluster love life, increase your chances of getting laid on Saturday night, or heighten physical pleasure. The main purpose isn't even sexual enjoyment or procreation. Having said all that, however, it's quite likely your intimate relationships and sexual satisfaction will improve as a result of practicing sex magic—that's just not the primary objective.

Don't get me wrong. Sex magic is a lot of fun. And yes, it can increase your chances of getting laid (I'll explain how in chapter 8) as well as heighten your pleasure. But it offers you much more than a good time. Its possibilities, in fact, may be limited only by your imagination.

Sex magic is a means to an end, a way to mobilize the creative power of sexual energy to generate a desired result. You engage in sex magic for the express purpose of causing an effect to occur in the manifest world or beyond. That's the fundamental difference between sex magic and ordinary sex.

The goal of ordinary sex, unless you're trying to conceive a child, is orgasm—and that's the end of it. But in sex magic, orgasm is just the beginning. As Jeffrey Tye explains in *Tantra: Sex Magic,* "the most powerful moment of human existence is the orgasm. Sex Magic is the art of utilizing sexual orgasm to create a reality and/or expand consciousness. All senses and psychic powers are heightened during orgasm. It is a moment when a window opens to the unlimited abundance of the unlimited universe."

Thinking Makes It So

Before we get into the nitty-gritty details about doing sex magic—and trust me, we will explore all sorts of delicious details—let's talk a bit about magic in general and how it works. Read the first paragraph of this chapter again. Your thoughts and emotions are the hammer and chisel with which you carve your reality from the raw material of the universe: energy.

Maybe you've heard of something called the Law of Attraction. Simply put, the Law states that you attract whatever you think about. "Each and every component that makes up your life experience is drawn to you by the powerful Law of Attraction's response to the thoughts you think," explain Esther and Jerry Hicks in their bestselling book *Money and the Law of Attraction.*

Twenty-five hundred years ago, the Buddha said basically the same thing: "With our thoughts, we make the world." In essence, what this means is everything we experience in our sensory world evolves from our individual and collective thoughts.

That's a rather awe-inspiring idea—not one you learned in science class or Sunday school—so let's take a few moments to examine the Buddha's concept. What he and the Law are saying is the car you drive, the clothes you wear, and the food you eat all emerged from your thoughts. So did your professional position, your family situation, your home, your role in society, your career, your health, and everything else you experience in your everyday life. All of these started as sparks of imagination in your mind and developed in accordance with your beliefs. "Your life right now is a reflection of your past thoughts," writes Rhonda Byrne in *The Secret.*

Planting Seeds for Your Future

If that sounds a little far-fetched, consider this analogy. Before a house can be built, someone has to imagine it. The architect's idea is the seed from which the house grows. So it is with your life situations. You imagined them, and the seeds you planted days, months, or years ago grew into your present reality. If you extrapolate this logically you might say, *Well, yes, I wanted to be a doctor so I went to medical school, did my residency, et cetera, et cetera.*

But the secret of attraction is both simpler and more comprehensive than that. It proposes that if you focus your thoughts and emotions on something you'll draw that thing to you—whether or not you *do* anything obvious, measurable, or physical to make it happen. Thinking, said the Buddha, makes it so.

We're thinking pretty much all the time we're awake—in fact, most of us think several hundred thoughts per minute. You have the opportunity to make those thoughts positive ones. If you think about all the good things you desire, you'll attract those good things. But if you keep thinking about the deficits in your life, you'll draw more of those deficits to you. Essentially, you are what you think. If your life is at a standstill, the best way to jump-start it is to change your thinking. Dr. Wayne Dyer often says, "When you change the way you look at things, the things you look at change." That's good advice.

If you work with oracles, such as the tarot or runes, you may have discovered that the outcome predicted doesn't always occur. That's not the failure of the oracle. The oracle responds to your thoughts and emotions at the moment you consult it. Because your future develops from your thoughts and emotions *right now,* the oracle shows the outcome that will result if you keep thinking and feeling as you do now. If you change, the future will change, too.

Now consider this. According to science, all matter is composed of molecules that, because of the energy imparted to them, are constantly in motion. Your desk may appear solid, but in fact it's a collection of unstable molecules with lots of space between them. Quantum physics has shown that when an observer focuses attention on moving molecules, they coalesce. Your attention actually encourages molecules to start hanging out together in a certain place, thereby setting up the conditions that produce matter. This means that you affect whatever you focus on—your attention causes things to happen.

That's the secret of manifestation. It really is that simple—and that amazing.

It's All in Your Mind

Magic is all in your mind. You don't need crystals or wands or other tools to do magic, although they can be useful accoutrements. Magic's key ingredient is focused thought, powered by emotion and will, and enlivened by spirit.

In essence, magic is the art of intentionally utilizing the principles of attraction (which we'll talk more about as we go along) to create an outcome, by harmonizing your will with the forces of the universe. According to Aleister Crowley, the most infamous sex magician in modern times, "Every intentional act is a magical act."

Just as there are many different ways to paint a picture or do yoga or make spaghetti sauce, there are many different ways to perform magic. No one way is better than any other. If you do it right, all magic works. In this book, however, we're interested in a very specific—and very effective—

magical practice that harnesses a potent creative force: sexual power. It's called sex magic.

Basically, all magic, from the earthy practices of kitchen witchery to the ceremonial magicians' eloquent rituals, operates according to the same rules. Sex magic is no exception. When you do sex magic, however, you kick things up a notch. You throw another log on the fire and fan the flames. Sex magic propels you into a mind-body-spirit experience. Your mind creates an intention, your body provides the fuel, and Spirit guides the result.

Why Sex Magic Is So Effective

To successfully perform magic of any kind you need a focused mind—and sex really focuses your attention. "Orgasm, by its very nature, requires your total participation," writes Margo Anand in *The Art of Sexual Ecstasy.* During orgasm you're utterly present, completely in the moment.

Altered States

Sex also produces an altered state of awareness. Ordinary, logical, analytical thinking isn't the best place from which to do spells. Magic draws upon the right brain, not the left. Therefore, magicians often induce trances or heightened states of consciousness through rituals with many carefully choreographed steps or through other practices such as meditation, breath work, or fasting in order to perform magic more effectively. In *Secrets of Western Sex Magic: Magical Energy and Gnostic Trance,* Frater U. D. writes, "Sex magic draws a great deal of its power from the fact that sexuality in general and orgasm in particular provide us with an ideal 'natural' Gnostic trance for magical workings."

Not to knock other magicians' paths or practices, but if given a choice of starving myself for several days, sweltering in a sweat lodge for hours, or having sizzling sex in order to heighten my awareness, which one do you think I'm going to choose? What about you?

Sex Charges Your Battery

Basically, you use sex magic for the same reasons you would do any other type of magic: to cause something you desire to happen. Your goal might be to promote healing or attract money or achieve spiritual enlightenment. When you add sexual energy, you increase the intensity of a magic spell. It's like adding more octane to gasoline.

"What makes sex magick possible is that all living systems have the capacity to store a charge of energy," explains Donald Michael Kraig in his book *Modern Sex Magick.*

Our bodies are like batteries. We're plugged in to the cosmic energy source and draw juice from it every moment of every day. Without that juice, we'd die. When you practice sex magic, you enhance this energy connection and boost your personal power. You suck up more juice. You charge your system. You rev up your potential for manifesting outcomes.

The Role of Emotions in Magic

Your emotions, in addition to your thoughts, play a crucial role in generating outcomes. Emotions provide fuel for your thoughts. An isolated thought in itself lacks the power to do much of anything. But intense feeling hones a thought the way a blazing fire tempers steel. Put enough emotion behind an idea and you forge a thought into an instrument capable of achieving great things.

Emotions and Health

If you want a concrete example of how thoughts and emotions affect your physical reality in the most mundane way, consider their impact on your health. Stress, as Charles L. Raison, M.D., clinical director of the Mind-Body Program at Emory University School of Medicine in Atlanta, points out, is "a contributor to all the major modern killers ... It's hard to think of an illness in which stress and mood don't figure."

What happens if you shift your thoughts and emotions to a more positive place? According to an eight-year-long study of 97,000 people, conducted by the Women's Health Initiative and published in the *Boston Globe* in 2009, happy people enjoy longer and healthier lives.

You can learn to change your thinking patterns just as you can train yourself to change any behavior. The first step is to be aware of your thoughts and to realize that you have the power to govern them, rather than allowing them to govern you. Try these experiments to become more conscious of your thoughts.

- Set a timer for one minute. Sit quietly and just observe your thoughts, without censoring, judging, or intentionally focusing on anything specific. Notice how many thoughts flit through your mind during that time. If you're like most people, your mind jumps from one thought to another and brings up dozens of random ideas about your work, your relationships, something you heard on the radio, what you'll have for dinner, and so on. How many of these thoughts are useful, original, or inspired? How many are simply replays of thoughts you've had a zillion times?

· Read a newspaper article about something unpleasant. Notice how your mind creates thought-forms and how your emotions respond to those thoughts. Almost instantly, you feel worse than you did only a few moments ago. Now read something positive or uplifting. Notice how quickly your emotions shift to a more upbeat tempo.

Now practice controlling and directing your thoughts. Your thoughts and emotions don't just produce effects in your body, they produce effects in every area of your life. Magicians know this, and learn to guide their thoughts and emotions in order to generate the results they desire. The more joyful your emotions, the stronger your power of attraction and your ability to draw positive circumstances to you.

· Whenever you catch yourself thinking something negative, stop and purposefully replace that bummer thought with a more cheerful one. Refuse to allow yourself to dwell on angry, discouraging, or frightening ideas. As Edith Armstrong put it, "I keep the telephone of my mind open to peace, harmony, health, love, and abundance. Then, whenever doubt, anxiety, or fear try to call me, they keep getting a busy signal—and soon they'll forget my number."

· Whenever you catch yourself worrying about something that might occur in the future, stop and bring your thoughts back to the present. In his bestselling book *The Power of Now*, Eckhart Tolle described the amazing power that exists in the present moment. As we discussed earlier, your thoughts and feelings in the present are what create your future, so make sure they're creating the future you want.

Yes, you *can* do it. It just requires practice and a little willpower. And willpower is what you're working to develop so you can perform magic more effectively.

Sex Makes You Happy and Healthy

In *Macbeth,* Shakespeare wrote, "sleep … knits up the raveled sleeve of care." The Bard could easily have substituted *sex* for *sleep.* We all know from personal experience that great sex can ease a troubled mind and leave you feeling all is right with the world. A 2009 study by the National Health and Research Council of Australia found statistically that women who enjoyed satisfying sex lives had a better sense of overall well-being, and experienced less anxiety and depression than women who felt unfulfilled sexually.

There's a clinical reason for this. During orgasm the level of endorphins—the body's natural "feel-good" hormones—in the bloodstream increases by about 200 percent. Now consider this in light of the principles of attraction and it's easy to see why sex boosts your potential for bringing good things into your life. The more intensely pleasurable your feelings, the stronger your inner magnet becomes, and the faster your thoughts and intentions will manifest in the physical world. The equation is a simple one: focused thought + exalted emotions = amazing attracting ability. Given that orgasm is the best and most intense feeling human beings can experience, it's easy to understand why sex magic is so powerful.

Consciously Creating
Circumstances in Your Life

As you've probably guessed, there's more to sex magic than simply bonking your brains out day and night. If that was all you had to do, no one would be poor or sick or unhappy. Sex magic is both an art and a skill. Like any art or skill, it requires learning certain techniques and then practicing those techniques to build up your magical muscles. But technique alone isn't enough, whether you're casting a magic spell or having sex—and especially when you're doing both simultaneously. You've got to spice things up with a generous amount of passion.

You wouldn't try to run a marathon without first learning to jog, and you won't become a first-rate sex magician without mastering the basics. Consequently, we're going to start with some fundamentals of magic and work up to the elegant and juicy stuff. In the process, you'll become a better magician and a better lover.

Maybe you already know a little about magic—or a lot. That's great. Feel free to skip ahead to the chapters that deal with specific areas you're curious about and want to explore, like how to make that drop-dead gorgeous hunk fall for you or how to look thinner without dieting (that's in chapter 8).

Still, it can be helpful to review the essentials periodically as a refresher. I've known more than a few magicians who could deftly enact all the steps of casting complicated spells, but failed to attract the desired results because they didn't follow one very basic rule: their heads and hearts weren't in sync with their stated goals. Also, it can sometimes be useful to get a slightly different perspective. I've read scores of books about magic, and I've learned things from every one of them.

What You Think Is What You'll Get

We all go around constantly—but not necessarily consciously—creating the circumstances in our lives. Most of the time, we don't realize it. Here's an example. A friend of mine is convinced that every traffic light he comes to will be red. I assume the lights will be green for me. It's no coincidence that most of time he encounters red lights, whereas I frequently drive from one side of town to the other without having to stop. It all boils down to this: What you expect and what you give thought to will materialize in your life. Your beliefs produce the results you expect.

Successful magicians never put their minds on things they don't want to happen. Maybe you're afraid you'll lose your job or your lover will leave or you'll get sick. If you worry about it enough and keep imagining the dreaded outcome, guess what? You signal the energy around you to start clumping up in a particular way, according to the mental picture you've created. In time, your mental picture manifests. What was inside your mind materializes in the outer world. *As within, so without.* (More about this in a minute.)

It works the other way, too. You can focus your attention to generate the results you desire. That's the purpose of magic—to use your thoughts to consciously and intentionally create circumstances. And that's what this book is all about—learning how to manipulate mental and sexual energy to manifest the outcomes you choose.

The Art of Visualization

Visualization is a key component of magic. The term, popularized by Shakti Gawain in the 1970s, means creating a picture of something in your mind for the purpose of producing a particular effect in the physical world. Let's use the architect metaphor again. If an architect expects a house to be built according to his intentions, he must first see it in his mind's eye—right down to the tiniest detail. When you work magic you do the same thing.

Maybe you want to get a new job. First, imagine yourself performing that job. Bring your senses and emotions into the scenario. Really feel yourself doing whatever you would do in that position. Enrich your vision with as much color, enthusiasm, and detail as possible. See yourself having fun, enjoying the work, and performing it well. Envision interacting with colleagues in a pleasant way, getting appreciation from clients, receiving a big paycheck, and so on. Picture the outcome you desire, not the steps along the way. Hold the image in your mind for as long as possible. Imprint your intention in the matrix. Imagine those molecules we talked about earlier assembling to create a physical form. What you see is what you'll get, so design your vision carefully.

But what if you can't visualize (or think you can't)? Dr. Martin Hart, with whom I coauthored the book *The Best Meditations on the Planet,* suggests you start by thinking about your own home. What color is it? What material is it made of? How many rooms are in it? Does it have a fireplace? A porch? If you're like most people, you can easily picture your home's features in your mind. So, guess what? You *can* visualize.

Cosmic Connections

Five thousand years ago, the Egyptian sage Hermes Trismegistus is said to have inscribed these words on a green stone known as the Emerald Tablet:

> *As above, so below.*
> *As within, so without.*

This ancient axiom reveals another secret of magic: everything in the universe is interconnected. You and I, the stars in the heavens, the animals, trees, rocks, and rivers here on earth are all entwined in an elegant energy matrix.

We may appear to be separate entities, but that's only an illusion we've been trained to see and accept. Rather, we're like zillions of shimmering threads woven together to form an infinitely large piece of cosmic cloth. And because everything intermingles in this cloth, everything affects everything else.

The Butterfly Effect

Perhaps you've heard of the "butterfly effect," which suggests that when a butterfly flaps its wings, it influences the winds around the world. We humans metaphorically flap our wings all the time with our thoughts, words, and deeds—and when we do, the effects ripple through the energy matrix of our universe, to the four corners of the earth and beyond.

Likewise, we can't avoid being influenced by what goes on in the heavens, as any astrologer will attest. Look at how the moon impacts the tides and human reproductive cycles. Notice how it triggers your own emotions. *As above, so below.*

Beyond the Limits of Distance and Time

This interconnectedness enables you to work magic, even at a distance. Just as e-mail connects you with people around the world and allows you to communicate with your friends in England or Australia, energetic links let you send and receive magical "messages" without borders or limitations. All you have to do is follow the threads in the cosmic cloth to whomever or whatever you wish to impact. Healing and hexes, blessings and curses, and thoughts of all kinds travel along these energy pathways at speeds far beyond anything NASA could comprehend.

Have you ever gotten a phone call from someone you were just thinking about? That's a common example of vibrational communication. Your thoughts zipped through the energy matrix and hooked up with your friend's thoughts.

Time isn't a hindrance either. Energy can't be destroyed, so vibrations remain in the matrix indefinitely. That's why psychics can read the past and the future.

Interconnectedness also lets magicians draw upon the energies of natural objects, as well as inorganic beings and otherworldly entities, for spellworking. You may not believe you have much in common with a bay leaf or a chunk of amethyst, but for millennia magicians have tapped the resonances of herbs, gems, and other substances to attract good fortune or repel evil. We still do, and we'll talk more about this later.

Like Attracts Like

The energy matrix that surrounds and permeates our world is abuzz with vibrations that emanate from everything within the matrix. Sensitive individuals can feel these vibrations—and with a little practice, you can too. Different things resonate at different frequencies. Rocks, for instance, resonate at a slower frequency than trees, humans at a slower frequency than angels. Even within the human community, people resonate at vastly different rates. As you develop your magical abilities, you'll learn to perceive and interact with various entities—physical and nonphysical—

vibrating at varying rates. You'll also learn to shift your own resonance to a higher level through sex and other practices.

Picking Up Vibes

Through the language of resonance, we communicate with each other instantaneously. Pay attention the next time you meet someone for the first time. Even before you speak or shake hands, you pick up "vibes" from that person. Your energy field (or aura) connects with that person's energy field and you exchange information. It's not only body language or pheromones you're reacting to— your exquisitely refined energy receptors are reading each other's resonances.

When you meet someone whose energy is similar to your own, you feel an attraction. We even describe it as being on the same wavelength. Whether or not you realize it, you draw people and circumstances based on synergistic energy relationships. You attract what's similar to you, at least at the level of vibration. Like attracts like.

I'm sure you've had the experience of meeting someone you felt you'd known all your life. Your similar resonances caused the instant attraction. But the matrix doesn't distinguish between "good" and "bad" vibes—it merely aligns the ones that match, which explains why bad things sometimes happen to good people.

Here's an example. A man I used to know was going through a difficult time and felt very angry, but he didn't know how to express his emotions constructively. As he walked home from work one evening after an extremely trying day, fuming about his troubles, a guy jumped him and beat him up—for no apparent reason. He had attracted a person whose resonance matched the angry energy he was projecting.

Tuning Your Dial to the Desired Frequency

The frequency of your thoughts and feelings must match the frequency of whatever you wish to attract. Think of it in terms of a radio signal. You can only pick up a signal being broadcast by a tower whose frequency matches the one to which you've set your dial. Want to hear *All Things Considered*? Unless you tune in to a station that broadcasts NPR and this program, that's not going to happen. The same holds true when it comes to getting what you want—if you set your dial for "country" you can't attract "classical."

Let's say, for example, your goal is to attract prosperity. You have to attune your personal resonance—your own unique "radio frequency"—to the vibration of prosperity. You have to think prosperous thoughts and act as if you were already prosperous. Ideas, words, emotions, and images all contain energy and produce results. If you feel needy and desperate, and constantly worry about how you're going to pay your bills, you'll send out poverty vibes instead of prosperous ones. Guess what you're going to attract?

In *The Secret,* bestselling author Jack Canfield explains it this way: "When you think a sustained thought it is immediately sent out into the Universe. That thought magnetically attaches itself to the *like* frequency."

If you desire a happy relationship, your emotional state must be joyful. If you're seeking wealth, you must be able to feel yourself relishing your riches. When you feel good, you attract more of what makes you feel good. Your joyful vibration draws people and circumstances that are also resonating at a joyful vibration. As Carol K. Anthony notes in her book *A Guide to the I Ching,* "Only he who remains inwardly free of sorrow and care can bring in a time of abundance."

Your Emotional GPS

Your emotions also let you know if your thoughts and actions are in sync with what you truly desire. When you feel good, you can be sure you're headed in the right direction. But when you feel bad, it's a sign your train of thought has gotten derailed. In *The Secret,* Jack Canfield writes, "Our feelings are a feedback mechanism to us about whether we're on track or not."

Whenever you notice yourself feeling irritable, resentful, envious, or hostile, stop and shift your emotions to something more positive. Yes, I know this is easier said than done. But when you realize your thoughts and feelings are active forces that generate outcomes, you know staying in a funk will only make matters worse. To raise your resonance to a higher level do something you enjoy—take a walk, work in the garden, listen to music. Watch a funny movie. Toss a Frisbee for your dog. Remember something pleasant from your past. Organize a "play list" of happy thoughts, so when you find yourself spiraling downward you can pull one up and reroute your emotions before you go too far afield.

Here's another technique, called recapitulation, for getting rid of unwanted thoughts. When a discouraging idea or memory pops into your mind—especially one that keeps annoying you again and again, without resolution—inhale and turn your head to the left. Hold the thought and any feelings related to it for a few moments. Then quickly turn your head to the right, and imagine casting the thought out as you exhale. Repeat as often as necessary—maybe even hundreds of time a day—until you free yourself of that thought.

Why Doesn't Every Thought Manifest?

If thoughts are the seeds from which our realities grow, why don't *all* our thoughts materialize? Millions of thoughts flit through your mind every day. But most of them are just teeny, tiny sparks that flicker briefly, like fireflies, and then disappear. They don't gain enough momentum to manifest.

Manifestation Mix-ups

Often thoughts *do* materialize, but not always in the way you expect. Here's an example. One morning I decided I'd like some fresh flowers to dress up my dining room table and set about manifesting them. When a colleague of mine stopped by for lunch, he handed me a package of chocolate chip cookies. "I considered bringing you flowers," he said, "but since this is a business meeting, not a date, I thought it would be inappropriate." See what I mean?

According to holistic medicine, physical illnesses begin in the mind and eventually manifest in the body. Of course, nobody sets out to intentionally manifest a disease. Yet coronary problems can stem from anger, disappointment, or sadness—the term "broken heart" isn't simply a metaphor. Cancer may be the embodiment of long-held resentment. In some cases, illness attracts what a person secretly desires (perhaps unconsciously), such as attention from loved ones or time off from work.

Lack of clarity and passion undermine your magical power, too. You've heard the computer term "garbage in, garbage out," right? Well, the same thing holds true for manifestation. If you're unsure about what you're trying to produce, the outcome will be garbled. If you're halfhearted in your attempts, you'll get insipid results. If you try to work on too many ideas at the same time, you'll either overload the system or scatter your forces in a dozen different directions.

Let It Go

What if you really, really want something fervently and you think about it night and day, yet it still hasn't happened? So long as you keep obsessing about your desire, you hold onto it and fix it in place. It can't grow. You're stuck. In *The Book of Awakening,* Mark Nepo writes, "As long as we clutch to one thing … our hands cannot open or reach for anything else."

Remember, you create what you think about, so if you keep thinking about something *as it is now* that's what you'll get. More of *what is.* Even if you're concentrating hard on the future you wish to attract, you're still holding on. You've got to let it go, open your hands, give it up, relinquish control, and allow the universe to take over. Strange as it may seem, you have to release your desire before it can materialize. It's like placing an order at a restaurant—after you've given your order to your server, you have to sit back and trust that the kitchen will fulfill your request.

As we've already discussed, magic is a means for manifesting your wishes, a method for molding raw ingredients (energy) into the forms you choose. There's really no limit to what you can achieve through magic. You can see, however, that some rules apply and you'll get better results if you observe certain guidelines—especially when you're working with the supercharged energy of sex magic.

three

Putting Sex Magic
in Perspective

Much of sex magic has been written and presented from a male point of view. In some cases, this perspective has turned women off rather than turning them on. As contemporary female magicians openly share their insights and experiences, our understanding of sex magic will surely expand and deepen, emphasizing love and intimacy as well as power.

This doesn't mean women have been less important than men in the evolution of sex magic or that sex magic benefits men more than women. Here's the good news, girls: female sex magicians are likely to receive more attention, adoration, and enthusiastic pleasuring than nonmagicians. In sex magic, the woman serves as the creative vessel who gives form to the energy raised during a ritual. It's the man's job to arouse her passion and infuse her with intention. The more prolonged and intense her state of arousal, the more magical power she generates. Extended foreplay, therefore, is encouraged in sex magic.

Male and Female Energies

Sex magic relies on blending male and female energies. When we speak of male and female energies, we're not referring to men and women. Everyone, regardless of gender, has both masculine and feminine energies. Same-sex couples can do sex magic as successfully as opposite-sex couples. Indeed, some magicians, including Crowley, believe homosexual magic acts hold greater potential than heterosexual ones because the possibility of reproduction is not a factor. You don't even need a physical partner to perform sex magic (more about this later).

Doing sex magic can help you get in touch with the energies operating in you, especially if you've suppressed or rejected your other-sex side. Some magicians recommend role-playing and assuming the opposite perspective in order to create greater balance, and by extension greater pleasure. If you're the one who usually initiates sex, let your partner take the lead and experience how that feels. If you tend to acquiesce to what your partner wants, state your preferences emphatically and see what happens. If you're usually a "top," try being a "bottom" for a change.

Dissolving Separateness

Sex can be seen as an attempt to dissolve the separateness and limitations inherent in physical incarnation. Intercourse is the closest we can get to merging with another human being and with the Sacred.

Many spiritual traditions teach that eons ago we split off from the Oneness of Spirit and became individual beings. The book of Genesis expresses this in the story of Adam and Eve's expulsion from the Garden of Eden. Our sense of isolation and our longing to reunite with Spirit is the root of human pain and suffering. During sex, we reconnect for a short time with the cosmic pulse of life. We glimpse our divine nature and our union with all that exists in the universe.

The divine essence that flows through each of us—not the ego or the intellect—is the source of magic. We are at our best as magicians when we push the ego aside and access the creative force that enlivens us. Orgasm enables us to do this. Thus, the French slang term "little death," which referred to orgasm, accurately describes the death of the ego.

As Paschal Beverly Randolph wrote in *Eulis! The History of Love,* "The nuptive moment, the instant wherein the germs of a possible new being are lodged or a portion of man's essential self is planted within the matrix, is the most solemn, serious, powerful and energetic moment he can ever know on earth."

Different Schools of Magic

Diverse peoples in different parts of the world, over many thousands of years, have developed magical practices that fit their beliefs, experiences, and locales. As a result, magic comes in many flavors. Ceremonial magic, hedge witchcraft, shamanism, chaos magic, and countless other styles exist. You'll find plenty of information about these practices and others in books as well as online. Depending on where you live, you might even manage to locate groups or circles of magicians who follow certain paths, or metaphysical centers that teach various types of magic. None is better than any other, although you'll probably find that some appeal to you more than others.

If you possess a flair for the dramatic, for instance, you might gravitate toward ceremonial magic. If you feel a strong affinity with nature, green witchcraft could be your forte. Cultural, biological, geographic, or religious factors might influence your choices. Do what feels right to you. Play to your strengths. Although some of my peers may disagree with me, I see no problem with blending different traditions and techniques. My own magical practice, for example, emphasizes Wiccan, Druid, and Celtic concepts, but I also add feng shui and southwestern shamanism to the mix.

Combining Sex Magic with Other Paths

Perhaps you've already found a path that suits you. That's great! The good news is you don't have to give it up in order to engage in sex magic. You can incorporate sex magic into pretty much any other belief system. Do you enjoy making talismans and amulets? By adding the energy of sex magic, you can increase their effectiveness (more about this in chapter 11). If you're into crystals, you'll find lots of ways to utilize crystals and gemstones in your sex magic work. Whether you subscribe to the formalized tenets of ceremonial magic or the free-for-all ideology of chaos magic, you can blend sex magic into your practice.

You Don't Have to Be Spiritual to Do Sex Magic

What if you don't subscribe to any particular school of thought? No problem. Anyone, regardless of ideology, can do sex magic. Many sex magicians do have some concept of a divine realm and embrace the mystical side of magic, but that's not essential. You can view sex magic as having a spiritual component or approach it strictly from a physical/psychological angle. In this book I share my ideas and experiences, as well as those of other sex magicians, but you don't have to agree with them. Take what you like and leave the rest.

Magic isn't static—it continues to evolve along with the people who perform it. Again, I urge you to explore, experiment, and above all enjoy. Your knowledge and experiences will pave the way for magic's evolution.

The Ancient Art of Sex Magic

Sex magic is perhaps the most maligned and misunderstood form of magic—and the one kept most secret. Although sex magic has been practiced since before recorded history and appears in the mythologies of cultures worldwide, religious persecution suppressed this ancient art long ago and forced it underground. Sex magic and mysticism have ancient connections, and mystical aspects often find their way into sexual acts regardless of whether magic is involved. But when sex-negative forces in Christianity, Islam, and other religions seized authority, they banned many time-honored magical and mystical rites, rituals, and celebrations. They drove a wedge between sex and spirit, between body and soul. Sex itself became vilified, viewed as unclean or wicked.

We can't trace a single, continuing tradition of sex magic through the ages. However, abundant evidence exists to indicate that for thousands of years people around the world have participated in mystical and magical sexual practices of various types. Stone Age statues of fertility goddesses, most notably the Venus of Willendorf and the Venus of Hohle Fels discovered in what is now central Europe, suggest our ancestors of more than 20,000 years ago attached totemic value to sex and reproduction.

The Celts

The early Celts engaged in sex rites as a type of sympathetic magic. By making love in the fields, they ritually blessed the land to heighten its fertility. Spilling their seed onto the earth represented sowing the seeds of crops, while the powerful creative energy inherent in the union of male and female forces nourished growth. Sexual revelry has traditionally been part of the festival of Beltane, celebrated on May 1 at the beginning of the spring planting season in Europe, Britain, and Ireland. The maypole itself is an obvious phallic symbol, signifying the penis of the God inserted into the body of the Goddess (earth).

Mesopotamians and Middle Eastern Cultures

Thousands of years ago, in numerous Mesopotamian and Middle Eastern cultures, temple prostitute-priestesses performed a special mystical-magical role. As representations of the Divine Feminine, they offered their bodies to be used in ceremonies that honored Her. According to Sumerian mythology, Innana, the goddess of sexuality, engaged in the ritual known as the "Sacred Marriage" with her lover Dumuzi. The ritual embodiment of God and Goddess, sometimes called "the Great Rite," is still performed in modern-day sex magic (see chapter 12 for details).

Babylonian priestesses also performed sacred sex rituals, for which men paid money—not as they would to a street prostitute, but as an offering to the Goddess, whom the priestess represented. Herodotus wrote that "Babylonian custom compels every woman of the land once in her life to sit in the temple of love and have intercourse with some stranger . . . After their intercourse she has made herself holy in the sight of the Goddess."

Ancient Egypt

In ancient Egypt, sex was integrally linked with mysticism and magic. Millennia-old images depict the sky goddess Nut and the earth god Geb constantly conjoined in sexual activity. Devotees of the Egyptian goddess Isis enacted rituals based in the myth that Isis used magic to create a false penis for her slain and dismembered husband Osiris, and brought him back to life.

The Egyptians, too, had their priestesses—usually noble women, not slaves or commoners—who engaged in sexual purification rituals. "The priestess takes upon herself the sins and transgressions of the man in the ritual of negation. In the Egyptian language the word, *negation*, pronounced negation but obviously spelled differently in hieroglyphics, meant semen or the essence of man. The word modernly means to cancel or wipe out," according to Sabrina Aset in *A Brief History of Religious Sex* (www.goddess.org). "In ancient cultures with matriarchal religions, sex was considered something ennobling and uplifting. Sex could take you closer to the Gods."

Asia

For 6,000 years, in many areas of Asia, a spiritual discipline known as Tantra has been used to achieve heightened states of awareness. As Kamala Devi explains in *The Eastern Way of Love,* "Sex is holy to a Tantric. It is worship … Tantric art, writings and religious rituals glorify sex." Part of Tantric worship involves joining masculine and feminine energies, traditionally represented by the Hindu deities Shiva and Shakti, in sexual union. Elaborate Hindu erotic carvings grace the Kandariya Mahadeva temple in India, built around 1050 BCE. The *shiva lingam,* Hindu's sacred stone, is often considered a sexual symbol.

Early Greeks and Romans

The early Greeks and Romans, the Kabbalists, Gnostics, and Sufis, as well as the aboriginal peoples of many lands, practiced various forms of sex magic and sacred sex rites. The Greek term *orgia*, from which we get our word "orgy," actually means secret rites or secret worship. Despite efforts by mainstream religions to eradicate it, this knowledge was handed down through the ages via art, oral tradition, mythology, and symbolism. Even some of our familiar holiday rituals, such as kissing beneath mistletoe, are rooted in early sex magic customs.

It's taken a couple millennia to unearth the secrets of sex magic. Like buried treasure, the knowledge has lain in wait for us to rediscover it. Occult societies and magical orders have guarded the secrets all these years and passed them along to a select few. Books that discussed sex magic often relayed information in code to initiates—Crowley used a system of degrees to describe various types of sex acts.

Now the time has come for this knowledge to become available to all who seek it. Some information may have been lost through the ages, but modern-day magicians continue to infuse ancient wisdom with new ideas, thereby enriching the whole. With the advent of the Internet, a wealth of material is now literally at our fingertips.

Aleister Crowley and the Ordo Templi Orientis

Much of today's Western sex magic bears the imprint of the notorious English magician Aleister Crowley (1875–1947). He's even credited with adding the "k" to "magic" in order to distinguish it from parlor tricks and sleight of hand. One theory suggests that because K is the first letter of *kteis,* a word used in mystical Asian texts for the female sex organs, Crowley intended "magick" to imply sexual content.

During his travels in India and Africa, Crowley learned sex magic from the Sufis and the Tantrics, and brought his discoveries back to Britain. There he began experimenting and expanding upon what he'd garnered. He integrated his experiences into those of the occult brotherhood *Ordo*

Templi Orientis (Order of the Templars of the Orient, or OTO), which he headed for a time before forming his own secret society called *Astrum Argentinum,* or Silver Star.

The OTO evolved from Czech and Austrian occultists, who endorsed sex magic and recreated a nineteenth-century version of the Knights Templar. Although the original Templars have been accused of attempting to stamp out sex magic in the name of Christianity, evidence suggests that they were responsible for bringing the knowledge of sex magic to Europe from the Middle East after the Crusades.

An American named Paschal Beverley Randolph (1815–1875) strongly influenced the OTO's tenets, too. An initiate of the Hermetic Brotherhood of Luxor and founder of the Eluis Brotherhood, Randolph wrote a book titled *Magia Sexualis* in which he described the sacred and magical properties of orgasm. The OTO's founders utilized the teachings outlined in his book, some derived from Eastern mystical and sexual traditions, and formulated a systemized practice of sex magic.

Throughout much of his flamboyant life, Crowley promoted sex magic and earned himself a reputation as "the king of depravity." He called himself "The Beast" and enjoyed shocking the stuffy, Victorian-era English with his outrageous behavior. According to many accounts, Crowley's methods were often manipulative, misogynistic, and exploitative. However, he is generally considered one of the greatest magicians of modern times, and the most significant contributor to the field of present-day sex magic. If you wish to learn more, his numerous books discuss his magical concepts and activities.

White, Black, and Gray Magic

Magical systems arise within historical, cultural, ethnic, geographical, and philosophical settings. Consequently, they are imprinted with the ideologies, social norms, and mores of the people who developed them. What one magician or group of magicians believes to be ethical or appropriate might not be acceptable to another. I suggest you trust your own instincts, instead of following someone else's dictates. If it doesn't feel right, don't do it. But if it sings to you, go for it.

What's the Difference?

So what's the difference between white, black, and gray magic? It depends on whom you ask. On *Boudicca's Bard,* Joseph Max explains, "Such dualistic concepts as 'white' or 'black' magic are not applicable to Chaos Magic, at least not in the sense of being good or evil … If [chaos magicians'] magic is 'black,' it is because it deals with that which is dark and hidden."

Usually your intention, not the methodology, determines the spell's shade. The following distinctions are accepted by many magicians, but not all:

- White magic is performed for the purpose of connecting with spiritual forces in the universe, in order to gain wisdom, insight, or enlightenment.

- Black magic is done to harm or manipulate someone else.

- Gray magic encompasses everything else.

Most spells fall into the gray area. That doesn't make them bad or even dubious. In fact, the reason most people do magic in the first place is to get something they want— a job, a lover, money, and so on. According to the above guidelines, so long as you don't hurt anybody else in the process, everything's copacetic. I wish to point out, however, that I have no idea where these distinctions originated. Subscribe to them if you so choose.

Is White Right?

You might know people who refer to themselves as "white witches," meaning they engage in a benevolent form of magic. They may be following in the footsteps of Gerald Gardner, who in the 1950s helped revive a type of witchcraft rooted in northern European and British Isles paganism. Gardner sought to portray his brand of magic in a positive light and to contradict the barrage of bad press that had been levied on witchcraft for centuries. To that end he formulated numerous moral laws for its practitioners, many of which modern-day practitioners still uphold. Chaos magicians, on the other hand, take a no-holds-barred attitude and essentially dispense with dogma and moral codes. They assert that nothing is true, and everything is permitted.

You've probably read or heard the magical equivalent of the Golden Rule, that whatever you do comes back to you like a boomerang, magnified threefold. The Wiccan Rede states it this way:

> *An' ye harm none, do what ye will.*
> *What ye send forth comes back to thee,*
> *So ever mind the Rule of Three.*

If that's true, it's a pretty good reason to use magic con-scientiously. However, you may side with Crowley's posi-tion: "Do what thou wilt shall be the whole of the Law." Ultimately, you'll have to decide for yourself what's "good" and what's "evil."

When we consider this according to the principle of attraction, another picture emerges. If you accept the idea that you only attract what's in alignment with your own intent and purpose—and your own resonance—there's really no such thing as "right" and "wrong." The terms "good" and "bad," "white" and "black," lose their meaning.

What Sex Magic Can Do for You

Because sexual energy is a supercharged energy, it pro-pels your ideas and intentions outward with tremendous force. It shifts your manifesting ability into high gear. The inherent creative nature of sexual energy enables you to birth your thoughts into the physical world, with amazing results. By raising and directing this awesome, innate power you possess, you truly can create the reality you choose and attract anything and everything you desire.

Sex Magic and Prosperity

Having said that, sex magic seems particularly well suited to certain purposes. The creative nature of sexual energy makes it ideal for creating not only babies, but virtually anything else you desire as well. Prosperity, for example. Remember, sex energy is life energy. It nurtures growth and expansion.

Here's an easy spell you can do using sex magic to increase your income. Close your eyes and imagine planting a coin in a flowerpot. Fill the pot with rich, fertile soil and water it. Envision yourself tending the "seed" lovingly. Soon, a money plant sprouts and grows bigger and more luxuriant every day. From its stalks blossom hundred-dollar bills. Each time you pluck one, another grows in its place. Now, hold that image in your mind while you engage in sex (any kind of sex, alone or with a partner). At the moment of orgasm, release the image so it can take root in the matrix. See your sexual fluids raining on the plant and nourishing it.

Sex Magic and Healing

You can also promote health and healing very effectively with sex magic. By engaging the life force and channeling it through your body, you boost your immune system's natural ability to repel disease. Additionally, you can use the creative power of sexual energy to encourage the growth of new cells, tissue, and so on. As the studies cited in chapter 2 showed, sex makes you happy, and happy people are healthier than unhappy people.

Wilhelm Reich, an Austrian-born psychologist and colleague of Freud's in the 1920s, considered himself a scientist, not a magician. Yet he clearly understood how to heighten and direct sexual energy to facilitate healing, and he wrote about it in his book *The Function of the Orgasm.* His research showed that when sexual energy became blocked in human beings, physical illnesses including cancer and arthritis developed. It's not surprising that among the most prevalent cancers in Western society today are those involving the organs associated with sex.

Expanding Your Consciousness

If you are open to the possibility, sex magic can take you beyond your earthly awareness and into heightened levels of consciousness. Perhaps this is the greatest benefit it offers practitioners. In this elevated state, you connect with the Source of All That Is, the power that inspires life on earth. You experience yourself and your partner(s) as more than human beings and come to see one another as embodiments of the Divine. You perceive the glorious truth of yourself.

You can also look at it from a psychological perspective. Many of us feel intensely drawn to people who display the qualities of our animas or animuses. However, the attraction we feel may have more to do with our projections than with our actual partners. We think we're in love with our mates, when in actuality, like Narcissus, we're dazzled by our own reflected beauty. As a result, we may demand that our partners fulfill our expectations and feel disappointed when they fall short.

Sex magic allows you to intentionally connect with your other-sex side and embrace it joyfully. While you're engaged in a sex magic ritual, your partner becomes the representation of your inner ideal. You have an opportunity to realize a part of yourself that ordinarily remains hidden, and revel your wholeness. This awareness enables you to take responsibility for your own happiness and remove the burden from your partner. You also discover that fulfillment isn't found in one "special person"—it lies within you. Therefore, all men and women have the potential to serve as vehicles for self-actualization. The challenge, of course, is to remain cognizant of the difference between the human being and the anima/animus you embrace during magical practice.

Why Magic Doesn't Work Sometimes

If you're baking a cake and include all the right ingredients, follow the instructions precisely, and time everything perfectly, your chances of success are pretty good. When you do a spell, however, your thoughts and emotions are more important than your ingredients or actions. You can *do* everything right and still not achieve the outcome you desire.

The single biggest impediment to success—magically or otherwise—is doubt. As Henry Ford put it, "Whether you think you can or think you can't—you are right." If you doubt you can kick a field goal or sink a putt, you probably won't. But if you truly believe in yourself, you can achieve miracles.

Tips for Successful Spellworking

The following six points will help you get the best results from whatever type of magic you choose to do:

1. *Be confident.* When you perform a spell or ritual, trust that the outcome you intend will manifest. Don't even entertain the possibility of failure. Remember, your mind is the most important tool in magic, and you'll attract whatever you focus your thoughts on, whether you want it or not.

2. *Be consistent.* Don't keep changing your mind. If you start out trying to manifest a beachfront vacation cottage, and then think maybe you'd rather have a getaway cabin in the mountains, the universe doesn't know how to respond. Pick a plan and stick with it.

3. *Let go.* After you've finished doing a spell, let the universe take over. Trust the universe to manifest your intention. Allow it to materialize your desires according to its own rules and schedule. Don't worry about how things are developing. Don't stand on the sidelines evaluating, calculating, and pressing for results. All that measuring activity suggests you don't trust the process. A situation can't evolve if you keep fretting about it. When you put a seed into the ground, you must step back and let nature do her thing. If you keep digging up the seed to check on it, it will never have a chance to grow. The same holds true for spells.

4. *Be patient.* Sometimes matters take a while to manifest. Several years ago I decided I wanted a romantic partner and put my request into the matrix. As it turned out, the man the universe deemed right for me at the time lived 5,000 miles away. He had to arrange a job transfer, sell his house, relocate from Hawaii to Massachusetts, and find me—even though he didn't even know I existed. The whole process took about eight months.

5. *This or something better.* Even if you're pretty sure you know what you want, you could be selling yourself short. Additionally, you may not be aware of all the possibilities or extenuating circumstances.

The principle of attraction works for large requests as well as small ones—the universe can just as easily give you a yacht as a rowboat. Therefore, it's a good idea to qualify your spells with the phrase "this or something better."

6. *Express gratitude for all blessings that come your way.* As you do, you open yourself to receive more and more blessings, until you have exactly what you want. Expect good things to come your way and be open to all types of opportunities. Keep a gratitude journal and each day write down something for which you're thankful. In particular, note when you receive something you'd set out to manifest. An attitude of gratitude raises your resonance and increases your attracting ability.

In sex magic, it's especially important to keep these guidelines in mind. That's because most of what you're doing may seem unrelated to what you intend to manifest. For example, having sex might not appear connected to healing your uncle who has cancer. You may even feel a bit guilty about enjoying yourself while someone you love suffers. However, when you look at things in terms of energy, it all makes sense. You're raising life-affirming energy and sending it to someone whose life force has been compromised. You're contributing to his vitality. Furthermore, as countless studies have shown, a positive attitude can work miracles. Therefore, by projecting your pleasure to your uncle, you marshal creative, beneficial forces to counter the destructive agents in his body.

So go ahead, indulge.

How Do You Know If Your Magic Is Working?

How can you tell if your magic is working? You'll start noticing synchronistic experiences occurring in your life. Things begin to fall into place effortlessly. So-called "coincidences" appear more frequently. Meaningful symbols and situations turn up with regularity. Helpful people show up when you need them. Everything seems to move you toward your destiny.

Recently I decided I wanted to earn more income "passively," without having to work for the money. Shortly after I'd done magic for this goal, I started seeing the number 11 everywhere I looked—on digital clocks, license plates, store receipts, and so on. Eleven is my lucky number, so I sensed something good was transpiring. Within a week, one of my publishers notified me that an e-book I'd written for her company had been selected by another company for print publication, garnering additional royalties for me. A few days later, another publisher contacted me about reprinting some of my out-of-print books; another wanted to include some stories I'd written in an anthology. These synchronicities assured me that I was on the right track and my intentions were manifesting in accordance with my desires.

Cautions and Caveats

I suspect you wouldn't be reading this book if you held a lot of sex-negative attitudes, or if you weren't already interested in magic. For most people, sex magic isn't the first step on the journey into the magical realm.

Some sources caution you not to explore sex magic until you're familiar with other types of magic. They rationalize that because sex magic is a particularly powerful form of magic, you should develop some skill before attempting it. Perhaps these individuals are well meaning and they're just trying to protect you. Maybe they have a legitimate point. However, self-appointed guardians have a tendency to become patronizing.

Is sex magic potentially dangerous? Sure. *All* magic is potentially dangerous. So is driving a car, but the only way you learn is by doing it. Every magician with whom I've discussed this has gotten burned a few times, just as every athlete I know has been injured a few times. You'll never find out what you're capable of until you try, and unless you "push the outside of the envelope" you'll never get beyond your self-imposed limits.

Sexual energy is neutral. It has no conscience or inherent moral quality attached to it, just as fire is neither good nor bad. A magician can use sexual energy for whatever purposes s/he chooses. You can attach any intention or any emotion to sex energy.

Earlier, I talked about the distinctions between black, white, and gray magic. Let me reiterate that these distinctions have been determined by human beings. I have no way of knowing if the higher forces agree about this or if frankly, they don't give a damn.

Science tells us that every action prompts a reaction, but more importantly, personal experience proves it. Pat your beloved cat and she'll purr. Slam your fist into a door and you'll feel pain. Do a spell to ensnare someone you're hot for and … well, I'll let you figure out that one yourself. The guidelines for sex magic are essentially the same as for any other type of magic except that, to use our car metaphor again, when you do sex magic, you're driving a Porsche instead of a Honda Civic.

four

Preparing to Do Sex Magic

According to Aleister Crowley, "Magic is the Science and Art of causing Change, on a material as well as a spiritual level, to occur in conformity with Will by altered states of consciousness." Magic, as we've already said, is a method for marshaling raw energy to produce the outcomes you choose by focusing your thoughts and emotions toward desired goals. So exactly how does that work? And what exactly do you do?

Rituals, Rites, and Spells

Magicians manipulate energy by performing spells and rituals. You could think of magic spells and rituals as patterns designed to help bring about the outcomes you desire, just as you might follow a pattern when knitting a sweater. They give structure to your intentions and guide you from step A to step B, and beyond. Magic spells and rituals serve three basic purposes:

- · They focus your mind and keep your thoughts from wandering.

- · They shift your mental state from ordinary awareness to a more creative level of consciousness.

- · They raise energy to empower your intentions and propel them out into the universe.

Rituals, rites, and spells may or may not involve people other than the primary magician. Often they include special clothing, food, tools, settings, music, recitations, and/or other accoutrements. Although technically, you don't need any of these things—your mind is what creates the magic— the more you can enliven your senses and engage them in the ritual or spell, the more effective you'll be. Just as atmosphere can add to your enjoyment of sex, atmosphere can enhance your magical workings. The point is to step outside your mundane world for a while and enter a place of wonder and mystery.

Rituals

Rituals are choreographed enactments comprised of a series of ordered procedures devoted to a particular purpose. The Catholic Mass is a good example of a highly formalized religious ritual. The secular world as well as the spiritual one embraces rituals of many kinds. Sporting events, for instance, are replete with rituals, from the singing of the national anthem to the halftime performance to the team handshakes at the end of the game. In our everyday lives we rely on rituals, too. Pay attention to how you conduct the stages of your day—your morning ablutions, commuting to work, the way you arrange your workday, your exercise program, preparing and eating dinner, getting ready for bed—and you'll notice a pattern of small, but significant rituals.

When doing magic, you can enact time-honored rituals or design your own. In the beginning, it's probably best to try some established and widely used rituals until you understand what serves your purposes and why. You'll find lots of books, including this one, that outline various types of rituals. Even if you follow the basic guidelines for a ritual, don't be afraid to add your own personal touches. Trust your instincts and do what feels right to you.

Rites

Rites—magical and otherwise—are special rituals that mark meaningful passages in life. Among our familiar rites we find baptisms, birthdays, bar mitzvahs and First Communions, graduations, weddings, anniversaries, retirement parties, funerals, and other milestones. Holiday celebrations fall into this category, too.

Spells

Most spells are rituals, too. They include a series of purposeful steps and often incorporate various ingredients chosen to enhance an effect and/or produce a specific result. A spell may be as simple as lighting a candle, making a wish, and then extinguishing the candle—a spell we've all done at birthday celebrations. Or it may involve an intricate series of movements, incantations, and other actions using numerous tools and techniques, and transpire over a period of hours, days, or weeks.

Magicians perform spells intentionally to generate outcomes, but nonmagicians frequently cast spells, too, usually without realizing it. Every time you cross your fingers for good luck or curse someone for stealing your parking space you're doing a type of spell. Many of the best spells, however, utilize the power of ritual to sharpen the magician's mind and strengthen the spell's effectiveness.

You may choose to perform rituals and spells on auspicious days that resonate with energies that support and enhance your purposes. Later on we'll talk about some of these powerful periods, including lunar phases and eight holidays called sabbats that make up what's known as the Wheel of the Year.

Creating a Magical Environment

Though strictly speaking you don't need any "frills" to do magic, the right atmosphere can certainly contribute to your success. If you've ever attended a professional theater production, you've seen how lighting, costumes, and set design enrich the drama of the play. The same holds true when you do magic. A dynamic environment that engages all your senses and draws you out of your ordinary, everyday world into the magical realm intensifies your emotions and thereby increases your potential power.

This is especially true in sex magic. In a sense, a sex magic ritual is a choreographed production, and props that set the right mood are encouraged. Perhaps you find that candlelight, risqué lingerie, perfume, sex toys, and other accoutrements heighten your pleasure and add to the overall experience. Great, use them. A man I know likes to wear mink earmuffs that stroke his partner's inner thighs when he gives her oral sex. A woman friend slips glow-in-the-dark ornaments on her labia ring. When you're doing sex magic, you want to pull out all the stops. The more heat you can muster, the better.

Outdoor Settings for Sex Magic

This preliminary exercise stimulates your imagination—and all magic starts in the imagination. Make a list of places you'd like to do sex magic. Write down some favorite places where you've already enjoyed having sex, as well as ones you've always fantasized about but haven't tried yet. Don't censor yourself—even if your ideas seem a bit over the top, just thinking about them may get you hot, and that's a step in the right direction.

Many Pagans feel a strong connection with Mother Earth and prefer to make love outdoors in natural settings whenever possible. Druids consider trees sacred. A shady spot in an oak grove could be a perfect place to do sex magic—or even in a tree itself, if you're agile. Any place where the four elements—earth, air, fire (sun), and water—combine will heighten and harmonize your energy. How about a private cove on the beach where the rhythm of the waves accompanies your own rhythmic movements? Or near the base of a refreshing waterfall? Or on a flat rock in the middle of a stream? I used to have a secret pond hidden deep in the woods where I took my lovers to work magic. My all-time favorite spot was on a rocky cliff ledge that jutted out high above the Aegean Sea.

Caves provide a wonderfully symbolic setting for sex magic, exemplifying the female body's own dark, damp cave. A canyon where water flows along a channel in the earth could simulate the flow of the life force up the spine and through the body's energy centers, known as *chakras*. If you have the opportunity, tap into the vibrations that resonate in such sites by making love in these places. Feel your body's rhythms naturally align with the earth's pulse. Notice how the terrain amplifies your energy and your physical sensations, just as it amplifies and echoes any sounds you make.

Liminal zones, where two different types of terrain meet, resonate with powerful energies, too. Consider a beach or rocky coastline, where land and water come together; the edge of a forest, where an open field merges with dense woods; the foot of a mountain, where flat land begins to rise steeply. Dawn and dusk, at the interstices of day and night, are liminal zones, too. All these "betwixt and between" places physically depict states of transition. Here the energies are quite fluid and malleable. If you want to shapeshift, journey to other realms of existence, or communicate with entities from other worlds, these are good places to work your magic. Spells to promote major changes and rituals that mark transitions in your own life can benefit from the energies present in these magical zones, too.

Labyrinths and stone circles amplify and focus energy. Since antiquity, magicians have enacted rituals and rites within these mystical shapes. Stonehenge, of course, is the most famous stone circle, but magic circles and labyrinths dapple the globe. For many years, I had a stone labyrinth in my backyard, where I conducted most of my magic spells and rituals. If your environment permits, you might want to consider building one yourself. The pathways in the more ancient, seven-circuit labyrinth connect to the seven chakras, the seven colors of the rainbow, the seven notes of the musical scale, and the seven planets visible to the naked eye—no wonder it's such a powerful and mystical form. If you decide to build a stone circle, position tall, phallic stones at the four compass points or nearby to balance the feminine, womblike quality of the circle.

Indoor Settings for Sex Magic

Next, list some places indoors where you'd like to do sex magic. Think outside the bedroom! It's okay to include spots you've already enjoyed and will revisit, but give your imagination free rein. If you have a fireplace, lying in front of it on a plush rug is an obvious choice. Bathtubs and showers, where you can leisurely soap one another's bodies, immediately come to mind, too. Window seats, reclining lounge chairs, barstools, and dining tables all offer erotic possibilities. A lover once deliciously turned me into a human ice cream sundae on the kitchen counter.

Also contemplate ways you can enrich the sensual ambiance of your indoor environment. Silk sheets feel fabulous against bare skin. Essential oils, incense, and candles entice your nose and eyes, enhancing the mood in any room. Play around with artwork, mirrors, and plants. Once a lover brought me an armload of roses, enough to lavishly adorn every room in my house and float rose petals in my bathwater. Again, the goal is to transform your mundane environment into a magical one.

In chapter 9 we'll discuss setting up magical environments in more depth and detail. For the time being, have fun fantasizing.

The Sex Magician's Toolbox

Like artists and skilled craftsmen, magicians employ special tools to facilitate their work and help produce the results they desire. Southwestern shamans use drums, medicine bags, fetishes, feathers, bones, and various natural objects in their magic. Feng shui practitioners favor red ribbons, crystals, wind chimes, and mirrors. The tools described in this chapter are popular in many Western schools of magic. What I want you to notice is the connections between the shapes of these tools and our reproductive organs—it's not a coincidence. Despite their shapes and symbolism, these tools aren't sex toys. You may consecrate your sex toys as magical tools, though, if you wish.

The Wand

The most familiar of all magic tools, the wand represents masculine energy, hence its obvious phallic shape. A magic wand should be at least six inches in length, but only as long as is comfortable for you to handle (more phallic implications). Often, the tip is flame-shaped and thicker than the shaft, like the head of a penis. In spells and rituals, the wand depicts the element of fire, the dynamic, assertive, *yang* force in the universe.

Magicians use wands to direct energy, not to turn guys into toads. Let's say you want to attract energy to you from another source, such as the sun or moon. Aim your wand at the sky, close your eyes, and envision yourself drawing solar or lunar power down to earth. Feel it rippling through the wand, along your arm, and into your body. You can also send energy through your wand to someone or something else. Point the wand toward your subject as you imagine energy shooting out the tip of the wand and connecting with your subject. The ritual of circle casting is often performed with a wand (see chapter 12).

Traditionally, magic wands were made of wood and carved or painted with meaningful symbols. That's still a good way to go, but if you prefer, choose a metal, glass, crystal, or ceramic wand. You can fabricate your own or purchase one ready-made. To emphasize the masculine nature of this tool, use the colors red or orange and/or the metals iron, bronze, or steel. You might also wish to adorn it with carnelian, red jasper, or other fiery gemstones.

The Pentagram

The pentagram symbolizes feminine or *yin* energy and the receptive, fruitful, nurturing element of earth. This five-pointed star represents the human body: head, arms, and legs. The circle surrounding it symbolizes wholeness, unity, and completion; it also suggests the entrance to the vagina.

One of the pentagram's main purposes is to provide protection, and many magicians wear pentagrams for that reason. You can also hang one on the door to your home or business to safeguard it. Dangle one from your rearview mirror to protect you and your car from harm. You might even draw or tattoo one on your body as an amulet. In a circle-casting ritual, a magician may draw pentagrams on the ground or in the air at each of the four compass directions. This shields you and the energy you raise during a spell or ritual from unwanted forces.

Silver, a feminine metal, is traditional for pentagram jewelry, but a pentagram can be made from wood, ceramic, cloth—just about anything. Some schools of thought, such as the Golden Dawn, describe specific sizes, colors, and materials for their practitioners' tools; others tend to be more flexible.

The Athame

The athame or ritual dagger, as its shape indicates, also represents masculine energy. Although the name's origin remains obscured in antiquity, it may derive from the Arabic *al-dhamme,* a Moorish ritual knife said to have been used for sacred offerings. The athame signifies the active, changeable, mental element of air. Usually, an athame is a double-edged knife about the length of an average penis; however, some Wiccans carry curved athames emblematic of the crescent moon.

Magicians banish unwanted energies by slicing them away with the athame. Before a ritual, wield it to repel forces or entities from the area where you'll be performing magic. Hold your athame in your hand and slash at the air within your ritual space, until you feel you've cleared it completely. You can also sever restrictive bonds of an energetic/emotional nature with your athame. If you like, you can use your athame instead of a wand to cast a circle. Don't cut food with it, though—save it for magical purposes.

An athame can be made of any metal, but steel, brass, bronze, iron, or gold, which embody masculine energies, are preferable to silver or copper. Although less common, bone, ivory, stone, or quartz crystal could be used for an athame. The hilt may be wood, leather, metal, or whatever material feels comfortable in your hand. Decorate it with magical, astrological, or other meaningful symbols if you wish.

A word of caution: before you acquire an athame, research its history. An elaborate antique knife might be attractive, but if it served as a weapon in its past life it may not be the right tool for your purposes. A few years ago, I found a handsome vintage knife that I thought would make a cool athame, until I learned it had formerly been used as a brith knife. Not the sort of energy I want to bring to my sex magic practice!

The Chalice

Shaped like a womb, the chalice or cup depicts feminine energy. It represents the flowing, receptive, life-giving element of water. The most famous chalice, of course, is the Holy Grail.

Usually the chalice holds potions or liquids served during a spell or ritual. Consequently, your chalice should have a longer-than-usual stem so it can be passed easily among participants. Don't drink ordinary beverages from it, only ritual brews and magic potions.

Your chalice may be glass, crystal, metal, ceramic, or even wood. I don't recommend plastic, though—too déclassé. If you choose a metal one, silver is preferable because of its feminine qualities. Some magicians suggest using a chalice shaped like a crocus flower and etched or painted with eight petals.

Candles

Candles symbolize the fifth element: spirit. A burning candle serves as a connection between the earth plane and the realm of spirit—the flame represents spirit, the wax shaft signifies earth. Among the most common and versatile of all magic tools, candles come in a wide range of shapes, sizes, and colors for various intentions. In chapter 9 you'll learn which to choose for specific purposes, and why.

Illumination is the most obvious use for candles. In mundane settings, candlelight infuses a room with mystery, elegance, and romance. The same holds true when you're working magic, especially sex magic. In spells and rituals, however, candles serve many purposes beyond illumination. They may represent energies, people, situations, or actions. They can launch your intentions into the matrix. They can honor a deity. The flickering flame can help to induce a light trance. According to feng shui, candles add vitality to a space and increase positive energy. Just as many of our religious and secular ceremonies include candles, virtually any spell or ritual can make use of them.

You can purchase ready-made candles or fashion your own. Check out the increasingly popular "healthy" candles made from beeswax or soy with lead- and smoke-free wicks. Scented candles entice the senses when you're doing sex magic—for best results, choose candles scented with pure essential oils that contain the energy of the plants from which they are derived.

Other Tools

After you've acquired the basics, you may want to include additional tools in your magician's toolbox.

- The sword, a larger version of the athame, has similar symbolism and uses. To simultaneously cast a circle and clear unwanted energies from your ritual space, hold a sword parallel to the ground, pointed outward, and walk clockwise in a circle around the area you wish to sanctify. Open the circle by repeating this action in reverse. Because of the sword's size and weight, men tend to use it more often than women do.

- The cauldron, like the chalice, is a vessel for magical brews and potions—it's perfect for cooking special soups and stews at rituals, too. If you don't have access to a fireplace or balefire pit, you can build a small fire in an iron cauldron for burning spells. A cauldron can also capture and contain sexual energy if you keep it nearby when you're doing sex magic. Choose a durable, cast-iron cauldron with three feet (representing the three phases of life and the three dimensions in physical manifestation) for concocting your magical brews.

- Bells and drums disperse unwanted energies. They can also be used to mark the steps in a ritual. Drums, gongs, and other musical instruments raise energy as well. Drums have long been used as communication devices. In Africa, the many drumbeats have special meanings that allow drummers "talk" to one another. You can communicate with someone (in this world or elsewhere) by holding your message in your mind while you drum. If you prefer, fashion a talisman, amulet, or other charm and tie it on your drum, or paint an image on the drum that symbolizes your objective. Each time you strike the drum, you'll propel your intention outward, toward your target.

· Knots tied in cords or ribbons hold energy until you decide to release it. In chapter 8, you'll learn how to capture sexual energy in knots and retain its power for future use. Knots can also bind enemies or disruptive forces. For example, if you feel threatened by someone, you may wish to create an effigy of that person and disempower it by tying its hands and feet.

· Crystals hold or direct energy. They also provide protection and lend their own inherent properties to aid your purposes. Crystal workers believe crystals and gemstones are actually life forms with innate characteristics and powers. Quartz crystals can be "programmed" to assist you in myriad ways. Various gemstones possess specific qualities that can empower your spells and rituals. Rose quartz, for instance, resonates with the energy of love; aventurine can augment prosperity magic.

· Incense, in addition to perfuming and purifying your ritual space, can be used to cast a circle (see chapter 12). Burning incense is also a way to send requests to the deities and invite them to join you in performing a spell or ritual. Because scent plays such a key role in seduction and eroticism, incense is an obvious accessory to include in your sex magic practices, too.

Choose aromas that stimulate your appetites, and/or represent your objectives.

· Oracles, such as tarot cards and runes, provide guidance, offer insight, and give you a glimpse into the future. You can also utilize their imagery in talismans and amulets to symbolize your intentions. When you're doing sex magic, these visual tools can help you to focus your mind on your goals. You might consider working with a pendulum, too, in order to gain insight into present and future issues.

· A *grimoire* or book of shadows is a magical diary in which you record your spells and rituals, as well as your thoughts and experiences. Keeping a log of magical practices is much like a cook writing down favorite recipes. Describe the ingredients and steps involved, as well as your outcomes—what went right and what went wrong. It can be helpful to date your entries and to include relevant factors such as the position of the sun and moon.

Caring for Your Magic Tools

Most magicians recommend clearing your tools before you work with them, to remove any unwanted energies—from someone else or the environment—that might interfere with your intentions. Simply wash them in tepid water with mild soap, then pat them dry. Or, hold them in the smoke of burning sage or incense for a few moments. Chalices and cauldrons must be washed every time you use them to prepare or serve ritual concoctions, but your other tools won't need cleansing again unless they're exposed to disruptive forces or someone else touches them.

Treat your magic tools as you would any prized possession. It's a good idea to store your tools in protective containers when they're not in use. Silk pouches or wrappings, velvet or leather bags, and wood or ceramic boxes prevent ambient energies from tainting your tools. (A ziplock bag would work, too, I suppose, but it's way too tacky.) Sheathe athames and swords when you're not using them, just as you would a hunting knife or fighting sword. Other than the chalice, which is shared during rituals, your tools should not be handled by anybody else, except perhaps a magic partner, and only with your permission. You want your tools to respond to your vibrations, not someone else's.

Many books, including my own, offer more in-depth and extensive information about fabricating, charging, and caring for your tools. (See Resources and Recommended Reading at the end of this book.) In chapter 11 you'll learn how to use sexual energy to charge your magic tools and imbue them with special power.

Magic Altars

An altar provides a center and focal point within your sacred space. Just as your desk is where you do much of your mundane work, your altar is the place where you do much of your magical work. However, your altar also serves as a link between you and the realm of Spirit. You invite higher forces to join you here to participate in your spells and rituals and to empower your intentions.

In some cases, the steps of a spell or ritual are performed in relationship to the altar's position. Because you begin casting a circle in the east, where the sun rises, some magicians recommend placing your altar in the eastern part of the area where you'll do your magic. Others advise centering it in your sacred space, so participants can easily move around it during a ritual. Do what's convenient for you—in a small apartment your options may be limited.

Setting Up Your Altar

Your altar could be an elegantly carved wooden cabinet, a bookcase, table, mantel, or shelf. Even a simple box draped with a handsome cloth or decorated with images and symbols that hold meaning for you will suffice. You can also display and store your magical implements in/on your altar.

If you choose to place your primary magic tools on your altar, set out all four of them to represent a balance of the four elements: earth, air, fire, and water. Position a pair of candles on your altar, too. Again, to establish balance, select a red, orange, gold, or white candle to signify masculine energy and one of blue, green, silver, or black to symbolize feminine energy. Fix them in fireproof candleholders and make sure to burn them safely. If space permits, you might wish to display other magic implements, flowers, statues, crystals, symbols, and so on.

During sex magic rituals, place sexually explicit or symbolic items, such as shiva lingam stones or erotic artwork, on your altar. How about a penis-shaped candle? To mark the seasons, change the altar cloth and decorations. For lunar rituals, position the altar so the moon's light falls on it, if possible. And just in case this isn't obvious, keep your altar neat and clean—dust, dirt, and clutter inhibit the flow of magical energy.

Creating an Altar for a Specific Deity

Let's say you want to petition for the aid of a particular deity. One way to attract a deity is to erect an altar to him/her. You can create a permanent altar in honor of a god, goddess, angel, totem, or other entity you wish to work with on a regular basis. Or, you can set up a temporary altar to draw upon the powers of a certain being for a single spell/ritual/objective.

First, purify the altar by smudging it with the smoke of burning sage. Clear away all items from the area that may not relate to or please the deity whose assistance you seek. For example, a Vila, the Eastern European protector of forest creatures, might not respond well to that stuffed deer head hanging over the mantel that your husband bagged on his last hunting trip.

Next, find an image of the deity—a statue/figurine, illustration, or other likeness—and display it on your altar. You can even download a picture from the Internet. If a specific symbol or object is associated with your chosen deity, you could place a representation of it on the altar, too. Because Diana is known as a moon goddess, you might include a depiction of a crescent moon.

Light a candle and some incense to dedicate the altar to the deity. State your purpose and ask him/her to help you in your endeavor. Be sincere. Trust that the deity you've solicited will indeed provide the aid you seek.

Outdoor and Portable Altars

If the opportunity exists, you might consider erecting an altar outdoors. Many ancient sacred sites around the world, including Stonehenge and Machu Picchu, feature stone altars where rituals and rites likely took place. A stone altar, either found fortuitously or constructed intentionally for your purposes, offers durability and longevity—like these famous examples, it could last for centuries. But a tree stump or even a picnic table can serve as an outdoor altar.

An outdoor altar lets you immerse yourself directly in the forces of nature and draw upon the power of Mother Earth. It can also attract nature spirits or elementals who can provide assistance (more about these beings later). Obviously, any symbolic items or representations you choose to attract a deity must be weatherproof or portable. Be careful with candles and other combustibles, too—setting the woods on fire won't endear you to beings here on earth or in the spirit realm either.

If you prefer, create a portable altar that you can carry with you into the great outdoors or when you travel. Cigar boxes are perfect for this. After smudging the box, decorate it with images that express your intention and will appeal to your chosen deity. Place a few basic tools in the box: a candle in a travel tin, a few cones of incense, a packet of matches or a lighter, a small crystal, a picture or miniature figurine of the deity, pen and paper, and anything else you consider relevant—and you're ready to do magic spells wherever you go.

Now it's time to start utilizing sex magic techniques to attract prosperity, health, love, career success—whatever you want in life. But you can't just read about it. Sex magic is *not* a spectator sport—you can't be an armchair magician. You've got to put your body on the line if you want to see results.

Creating a
Magical Child

S exual energy is life energy. Its nature is to create. In the
most rudimentary sense, the union of male and female
spawns a physical child. However, every sexual act creates a
"child" on the spiritual plane, regardless of whether a flesh-
and-blood baby is produced on the material plane.

During sex, you plant "seeds" with your thoughts in
the fertile "womb" of the cosmic matrix. You impregnate
the matrix with what's known as a *magical child*. Essentially, a magical child is an etheric pattern that contains
the raw ingredients and the knowledge to evolve into a
specific outcome, just as an acorn contains everything
necessary to grow into an oak tree. Some sources describe

magical children as spirits or nonphysical entities whom you charge to carry out a particular purpose.

Hugh B. Urban, in his book *Magia Sexualis: Sex, Magic, and Liberation in Modern Western Esotericism,* expresses it this way: "For if ordinary, natural, undirected sexual intercourse can give birth to a new living being—a fairly miraculous thing in itself—then it is not terribly difficult to imagine that ritualized, intentional, willfully directed intercourse might give birth to effects of a supernatural, magical, divine (or demonic) character."

Regardless of how you choose to view them, magical children are the products of your thoughts and emotions at the moment you experience orgasm. You create them whether or not you intend to or realize you're doing it. If you aren't consciously directing your energy, you'll still create a magical child by default—and it may not be one you'd like to have in your life.

Take a moment and try to recall what you were thinking and feeling the last time you had sex. Were you intent on sharing a sacred union with a partner whom you viewed as an earthly representation of the Divine? Or were you hurriedly going through the motions, hoping you wouldn't miss too much of the football game? Did you feel love, joy, and true intimacy with your partner? Or were you stressed out, angry, bored, needy, asserting dominance, or just seeking release? Now imagine a child who would embody and express your thoughts and emotions at that time. Think about the magical children you've birthed in the past—and the ones you'd like to create in the future.

Establishing a Telos

Your thoughts and emotions are your direct link to the creative power of the universe. In his book *The Evolution Angel,* Dr. Todd Michael explains that what we call angels are "extensions of your own thoughts." Thoughts and prayers, he says, "are direct extensions of the Divine mind. These extensions live—they germinate, they grow, they take form, and they change things." The same holds true for magical children.

What outcome do you want to produce through magical means? Remember, creation at the level of spirit precedes manifestation in the physical realm. Whatever you wish to grow in your material world—prosperity, health, love, success—you must first plant in the spirit world using your thoughts and emotions.

During your lifetime you have zillions of opportunities to sow the seeds that will become your reality. Every time you have sex—any type of sex that results in orgasm, with or without a partner—you put in place an imprint that will develop in accordance with natural and spiritual laws.

Agree on Your Objective

Before engaging in sex, magicians decide on a *telos,* an objective they intend to bring about. *Merriam-Webster's Collegiate Dictionary* defines telos as "an ultimate end," originating from the Greek *tellein*, meaning to accomplish. Your telos might be to get a better job, ace a test, or resolve a problem with a loved one. Choose only one objective at a time so you can direct your undivided attention toward it. When your body's zinging like a slot machine with a winning combination, it's hard enough to focus your mind on your intention. This is not the place to multitask!

If you are working with a partner—or a group of people—discuss your telos in advance, and make sure everybody agrees on the result you intend to generate. If each of you has a different agenda, the outcome you produce will likely be garbled. Your conflicting intentions might even block or neutralize one another's—neither of you will get what you want. Contradictions in your own thinking interfere with the attainment of your individual goals. The same thing happens when you and your magical partner hold contradictory ideas or objectives during sex.

Keep It Simple

You may want to write down your telos, just to make sure you're completely clear about your intention and have all your bases covered. Writing your intention can help you refine as well as define your goal. Share what you've written with whoever will participate in the sex magic act. Your partner(s) may notice important details you missed.

Here's an example: A friend of mine wanted to attract a romantic partner and carefully described the qualities she sought in a mate. However, she forgot to include that her beloved be available and able to enter into a primary partnership with her. Before long she met the man of her dreams. Unfortunately, he was married to someone else.

Compose your telos in the form of an affirmation. An affirmation is a short, positive sentence stated in the present tense, as if the condition already exists. Let's say you intend to heal a stomach ailment. Your thoughts should address the outcome you desire, not the present situation you wish to change. Avoid negative words or focusing on the problem, as in this statement: "My stomach doesn't hurt anymore." Instead, use an affirmation like: "I am healthy in body, mind, and spirit." See the difference?

What if you aren't sure about all the specifics? Maybe you want to land a wonderful new job, but you don't know exactly what you'd like to do or even what's available. You could word your telos this way: "I now have a job that's perfect for me." This allows your higher awareness, which has a broader perspective and knows what's right for you, to align you with the best possible situation.

Keep it simple. Think short and sweet. Your telos should be something you can easily hold in your mind (and perhaps shout out loud) when you're in the throes of ecstasy.

The Power of Words

Perhaps you can distill your telos down to a single word, such as love, prosperity, or health. If your objective is to gain spiritual wisdom or guidance, you might call out a god's name to request that deity's assistance. If you're looking for a life partner, emphatically saying the word "love" while connecting with loving feelings—including self-love—will bring more satisfactory results than a detailed tally of the characteristics you desire in a mate. Yes, I know it can be hard to feel desirable and loved when the only sex partner you've had in a year is a vibrator. But don't succumb to self-pity and loneliness—you know where that leads. In Donald Michael Kraig's *Modern Sex Magick*, Tara writes, "All sex toys should be honored and treated as ritual magical objects within which the animus resides."

You Create as You Speak

Magicians often intone certain words during spells and rituals. When you speak, your words produce resonances that echo through your body and the cosmic matrix, impacting both. Dr. Alfred Tomatis, a French eye, ear, and nose specialist known as "Dr. Mozart," discovered that the sound frequencies contained in the upper ranges of the speaking voice can aid healing. Meaningful words, sounds, or phrases known as *mantras,* such as those used in Transcendental Meditation, cause measurable effects in brainwave activity and can induce altered states of consciousness. These altered states are a better place from which to work magic than ordinary, everyday consciousness.

Words—especially when spoken with clear and passionate intent—can generate results in the material world. The Judeo-Christian *Genesis* story says, "In the beginning was the Word." According to this account, the words God spoke led to the creation of the earth and everything on it. "Abracadabra," a word people often connect with magic, comes from the Aramaic *Avarah K'Davarah.* It translates, "I will create as I speak."

In the late 1980s, Japanese scientist Masaru Emoto studied the impact of words on water. He discovered that words—whether they were spoken, written, or simply thought—could alter the water's molecular structure. Words such as love, peace, and gratitude caused the water to form into lovely snowflake-like shapes when frozen, whereas expressions such as "I hate you" produced ugly, distorted forms. Considering that water comprises about 60 percent of our bodies (and about 70 percent of our brains), these studies indicate that words may influence our own health, happiness, and well-being. The old rhyme "sticks and stones may break my bones/but words will never hurt me" may be fundamentally wrong. (You can read more about Emoto's findings in his books *Messages from Water* and *The Hidden Message in Water.*)

Tuning Your Resonance with Words

Some magicians prefer to use chants or incantations. Incantations (rhyming affirmations), because of their catchy rhymes and rhythms, are easy to remember. The repetitive nature of a chant raises power and shifts your consciousness from the mundane to the magical realm. Chanting can be especially effective if you're working with a group. It paces the action, focuses the participants' thoughts, and builds energy, in the same way a group of sports fans chanting in unison does. Chanting the anti-war slogan "Peace Now," for instance, could be a good choice if your goal is to resolve a family feud or to send peaceful vibrations to a nation in turmoil.

Sometimes during group sex magic, one person or a couple will be designated as the primary magician(s). The other participants devote themselves to generating positive energy for the primary magician(s) to use. Producing a joyful noise by chanting or singing is one way to stimulate excitement.

The next time you're having sex—with a partner, a group, or alone—experiment with chanting to see how it affects you. You might choose to repeat a phrase such as

"I love you" or a word that holds special meaning for you. Some people like to intone words in languages other than their own, such as *shima* (pronounced shee-mah), the Hopi word for love, and focus on the sounds rather than the meaning. Even uttering "yes, yes, yes…" helps bring you to a state of optimism and acceptance. Notice how your energy shifts, how your heart opens, and how your emotions lift.

Remember, you can only attract people, situations, and things that match your vibration—the energy you are resonating with and emitting at any particular time. That's why magicians advise you to speak only about what you wish to draw into your life. Don't grumble about your problems—aches and pains, your spouse's shortcomings, money woes—you'll only attract more of the same. Instead, talk about the outcomes you intend to produce, the things you desire to manifest in your life. Combining the creative power of thought with the vibration of spoken words can activate profound results—especially when those words are passionately shouted out during moments of ecstasy.

A Picture Is Worth a Thousand Words

Long before the advent of writing, our ancestors used images to convey ideas. Some symbols transcend time and place—we find them in ancient cultures as well as modern ones, and they mean essentially the same thing to people around the world. When you're creating a telos, the old saying "a picture is worth a thousand words" holds true. Images can generate results even more effectively than words. That's because your subconscious understands the language of symbols, myth, and metaphor better than English, Spanish, French, or any other spoken tongue.

The left side of the brain deals with words. The right side of the brain—the part associated with creativity—works with pictures. Artists and other creative people tend to utilize the right-brain more than less creative types do. Because manifesting outcomes is all about creativity, it makes sense to stimulate the creative parts of your mind as much as possible. That's one reason many inspirational teachers suggest displaying photos or other images that represent your objectives on "vision boards."

Pictures Trigger Emotional Responses

Another good reason to use images in magical work is that they generate emotional responses that can nourish manifestation. We react immediately to pictures without translating them into words or analyzing our reactions. When you see a heart, you process *love* without ever thinking the word. Advertising research indicates that if images depict something different than what's being said—as in TV commercials for pharmaceuticals that portray happy people while a voice-over lists the drug's unwanted side effects—viewers will react emotionally to what they see, not to what they hear. Your subconscious, too, responds more readily to pictures than words.

As we discussed earlier, the principal tools magicians use represent male and female energies and are shaped like the sex organs. This suggests sex is such a powerful force—and so highly valued—that magicians choose to incorporate it symbolically into their most prized and personal magical implements, and to draw upon this force when they work magic. Magicians employ all sorts of other symbols and imagery to produce outcomes. Later in this book we'll go into more detail about various ways you can use imagery during sex magic to strengthen the power of your spells.

Avoiding Ambiguity

Words can sometimes be ambiguous or convey more than one meaning. Consider, for instance, the words "bear," "close," "fine," "lead," and "refuse." Each of these words can be interpreted in at least two distinctly different ways.

Unfortunately, many sexually explicit words have taken on derogatory connotations that have nothing to do with their real meanings. "Fuck you," for example, conjures up angry feelings rather than the pleasurable ones associated with the act itself—if you tell someone to "get fucked," you probably aren't wishing him a good time. We often use the words "prick," "dick," "pussy," "cunt," and "asshole" to berate or belittle someone, thereby linking loathing with the parts of our bodies that bring us pleasure. Talk about mixed messages!

In sex magic, images offer yet another advantage. You can look at a picture and subconsciously grasp its meaning, even if you're too blissed out to remember your own name.

Bridging Body and Spirit

Everyone agrees that we owe our physical existence to the creative nature of sexual union. However, many magicians, metaphysicians, and mystics look at earthly incarnation from a somewhat different perspective than biology does. This view suggests that you chose to be born into a particular body, family, life situation, and so on, in order to fulfill specific intentions you determined for yourself before you entered life on earth. Your desire to live on planet earth prompted your birth. This means that you have not only created everything around you and every situation in your life, you even created yourself as a human being. Your wish to exist in the physical form attracted people who offered their own physical forms to fulfill your intention. You instigated your own existence. The idea turns the theories of both Darwinist evolution and Christian creationism on their heads.

We are creative beings and our purpose for living on earth is to create. That's why artists, musicians, and other creative people feel joyful, alive, and purposeful when they are doing their art. When you are in a joyful state, doing something you love and feel passionate about, your creative power increases. Your resonance expands and your magical ability becomes stronger. Essentially, that's the theory behind Marsha Sinetar's bestselling book *Do What You Love, the Money Will Follow.*

In their book *The 7 Secrets of Synchronicity,* Trish and Rob MacGregor explain it this way: "When we are focused, passionate, pushing our limits, our brains release endorphins [the "feel-good" hormones]. Research indicates this happens during sex and childbirth, strenuous exercise, meditation, and intense creative work. If you visualize what you want when endorphins are rushing through you, desires manifest more quickly. It's as if the endorphins somehow help connect you to the powerful source of who you really are, and the potential of who you can become."

Writing into Being

Years ago, long before I knew about sex magic or the principles of attraction, I noticed that what I wrote about in my novels and stories often transpired in my everyday life. It turned out that I wasn't the only writer who'd experienced this. Along with several fellow authors, I gave a series of talks about the phenomenon, which at the time perplexed and fascinated me. I called it "writing into being." Now, of course, I realize that writing contains all the elements necessary for magical manifestation. The author envisions a situation, fuels the vision with joyful emotion, spends a great deal of time focusing thought on the process—and *voilà*.

Now that I understand the connection, I wrote an erotic novel in 2009 titled *Tarotica* (under the pseudonym Amber Austin), in which I intentionally blended the creative powers of writing and sex to produce results. Part of the story takes place at a fictitious winery in the Texas Hill Country. Not long after Ravenous Romance published the novel, I landed a job (without any previous experience or education) at a winery located in the very town I'd written about—the winery even looked exactly like the one in my book, even though I hadn't seen it before I wrote the book.

You might like to try this technique yourself. Don't worry about penning a Nobel Prize–winning novel, just describe in rich detail a situation you'd like to attract. As you write, try to see the action unfolding as if you were watching it on a movie screen. Fully engage your feelings in the process. Have fun. See what happens.

The Union of Matter and Spirit

Sex bridges body and spirit. It dissolves the ordinary limits of corporeal existence and gives you a glimpse of your true, infinite, and numinous essence. Some of our most enduring symbols visually depict the creative union of male and female, spirit and matter. The vertical line in the cross, for example, represents masculine energy and spirit; the horizontal one signifies feminine energy and earth. The Star of David, too, portrays this union. The downward-pointing triangle is the alchemical symbol for the feminine element water and the upward-pointing triangle is the symbol for the male element fire. Creation on the earth plane results from the intersection of both forces.

The *Thoth Tarot* deck, designed by Aleister Crowley and painted by Lady Frieda Harris, includes an interesting card in addition to the usual seventy-eight found in most tarot decks. The image on this card—a uniquely configured six-pointed star in the seven colors of the rainbow with a golden, five-petaled flower in the center—is a symbol for sex magic.

Reb Hayim Haikel, an eighteenth-century Hasidic master, puts yet another spin on the sex-creation connection. His chicken-or-egg concept suggests, "Creation was for the purpose of lovemaking. As long as there was only oneness, there was no delight." In other words, we emerged out of the realm of spirit into our physical bodies *precisely so we could enjoy the pleasure of sex.*

Creation vs. Procreation

Procreation, as we discussed earlier, is not the primary purpose for engaging in sex magic—although magicians may, and do, intentionally conceive biological children during sex magic rituals. Many sex magicians believe stronger magic results when reproduction is not the goal. Creative energy can then be channeled into generating magical children for other types of outcomes.

On *Rob's Magick Blog*, Robert A. Peregrine offers this idea: "The most basic and common use of exploitation sexual magic is the combination of the masculine ability of creation with the feminine ability of union which results in creating a child in the image of oneself... In contrast to exploitation sexual magic, equality magic seeks not to create a child in the image of self, but rather to rather to recreate oneself through union with another."

Crowley believed that "any form of procreation other than normal is likely to produce results of a magical character." This view led him to focus on such practices as homosexual intercourse, masturbation, and bestiality. However, Crowley was a notorious misogynist and a provocateur who took bad-boy glee in tweaking the uptight Victorian English, so consider the source when assessing his ideas.

Joshua Geller, writing on www.spiritual.com.au, proposes that you can reach high levels of magic by confronting your personal sexual taboos, barriers, and inhibitions, and by pushing beyond your own self-imposed limits and engaging in the very acts that challenge you. Other magicians suggest that nonreproductive sex, particularly sex with someone of your own gender, is inherently more equal and egalitarian than intimacy with someone of the opposite sex—especially for women, given our world's long history of male dominance and gender-oriented imbalances.

My own theories about the power of sex magic to successfully manifest outcomes in the physical world are more in line with those of Margo Anand. In her book *The Art of Sexual Ecstasy*, she writes, "When the sacredness of sexual union is felt, it is possible to experience your connection to the life force itself, the source of creation. This connection lifts your consciousness beyond the physical plane into a field of power and energy much greater than your own."

From that place of power, anything and everything is possible.

Sex Magic Partners

The nature of sex magick, whether one performs such magick alone or with partners of the same sex or the opposite sex, is that of working with polarities," writes Donald Michael Kraig in his book *Modern Sex Magick.*

You've heard the expression "opposites attract." That's what we mean by polarity: two opposite yet equal forces or energies that complement one another, so that when joined they form a whole.

Yin and Yang

Consider the Chinese *yin-yang* symbol. The black side represents *yin,* or feminine energy; the white side represents yang, or masculine energy. When the two halves come together they create a circle, the symbol of unity, completion, and wholeness. The same thing can be said of sex—sex is the union of opposites, when two become one. In Tantra, this merger of male and female energies is called *sakti,* a Sanskrit word that means "power."

Polarity naturally engenders dynamic tension, as the two opposite forces confront one another—and that translates into excitement. Think of a thunderstorm, which occurs when two different weather systems—a high-pressure front and a low one, or a warm front and a cool one—bump into each other. Look at the amazing energy generated by this meeting of opposites. That's what you're aiming for when you do sex magic. You want to raise a tremendous electrical charge that will zap your telos with a zillion volts.

Although sexual polarity is most obvious in a relationship between a man and a woman, polarity also exists in same-sex couples. We're talking energies and archetypes here, not anatomy. Masculine and feminine energies abide within each of us, regardless of gender. Swiss analyst C. G. Jung called them the *anima* and the *animus,* the unconscious female side of a man and the male side of a woman, respectively. Often, a person you find attractive embodies the qualities of your anima or animus.

Look at the yin-yang symbol again. Within the black side you'll notice a white dot, and within the white side is a black dot. Even in heterosexual partnerships, the woman may enact the "male" role (assertive) while the man plays the "female" role (receptive), during sex and/or in other areas of their lives.

Vive la Différence

In sex magic, the greater the polarity, the greater the energy charge. You want to accentuate, even exaggerate, the differences between you and your partner to heighten the excitement. Clothing, scent, movements, sounds, and so on can help you achieve this. If you've ever seen a Japanese *kabuki* drama, you've witnessed an intentionally exaggerated and stylized depiction of masculine and feminine.

You may enjoy trying something similar yourself. If you're a woman who usually wears jeans, corporate-world business suits, or "sensible" clothing (read L.L. Bean practical), don a pair of stiletto heels and a tight, low-cut dress for a change. If you're a preppy sort of guy, ditch the chinos and Izod shirt in favor of black leather or cowboy duds. Yes, you may feel a little silly or uncomfortable at first, but put the "inner judge" on hold for a while and get into the spirit of role-playing. Pretty soon you might find a part of you emerging that you didn't even know existed—and you might get off on it.

Polarity and Equality

When I suggest emphasizing the distinctions between male and female, I don't mean going back to the bad old days of patriarchy. I'm not recommending "Me Tarzan, You Jane" (unless that works for you). Equality is inherent in polarity. If you look at some of those old, pre-feminist movies you'll realize the sizzle between Lauren Bacall and Humphrey Bogart, Liz Taylor and Richard Burton came from juxtaposing powerful female and male characters. You need equally strong energies of both kinds to produce a magical thunderstorm.

When you're doing sex magic, you might also want to experiment with alternating sex roles, sometimes expressing one energy, sometimes the other. Doing so can help you understand yourself, your subordinate/repressed desires, and your partner as well.

Ultimately, you're striving for balance by merging the two extremes. You're seeking wholeness through the union of disparate energies. Sex offers a way to connect with your own anima or animus. The more cut off you are from yourself, the more compulsive your need for sex is likely to be. In part, the desire to join with another person is the desire to connect with the opposite-sex part of yourself and achieve inner harmony. For a brief time, sex lets you transcend the isolation of physical existence and dissolve your separateness into the Oneness of Spirit.

Attracting a Magical Lover

How do you go about finding a magical lover? If you're already part of a community or circle of magicians, or if you live in a place like Salem, Massachusetts, your search might not be all that difficult. However, the usual meeting spots, e.g., your workplace, the local pub, or Match.com, may not yield the best prospects.

Magical lovers can appear in your life in unexpected or unusual ways. I was fortunate enough to have one literally show up on my doorstep. The best way to attract a partner is to put out a call for someone who's right for you. Your thoughts and emotions draw people to you, and no one comes into your life unbidden. Therefore, anybody who knocks on your door or bumps into you at the supermarket does so at your invitation. By sending out a mental message, you can save yourself a lot of time going to singles' events or browsing computer-dating sites.

Send Out a Magical Invitation

Start thinking about the person you'd like to attract. What qualities do you desire in a partner? Consider physical, emotional, intellectual, professional, financial, social, spiritual, and other factors that are important to you. Spend time each day imagining your relationship with this individual. Envision yourself enjoying this person's company. Keep a journal about the future experiences you'll share, the things you'll learn from each other, the happiness you'll bring to one another. Get all your senses involved. Feel the excitement and pleasure of being intimate with this person. Use your sexual energy to empower your intentions. Do some solo sex magic and, at the moment of orgasm, propel your wish into the universe.

As mentioned before, you can only attract someone whose resonance matches your own. If you feel good about yourself, if you believe you are worthy and wonderful, you'll attract someone who thinks so, too, and who will support that vision of yourself. Conversely, if you're feeling needy, inadequate, and undesirable, the person you attract will reinforce those beliefs. You can only attract what matches your current vibration. If your *current* vibration isn't as high as the situation you desire, you might opt to spend some time raising your own resonance before putting an ad in the cosmic personals. Then you can draw to you the magical lover you truly want.

Romantic Partners and Magical Partners

Perhaps you're already in a relationship. Is your present mate the right magic partner for you? Maybe yes, maybe no. What's the quality of your relationship with this person? Do you share love, respect, passion, joy, acceptance, support, and commitment to one another? Or is there a lot of conflict, resentment, jealousy, mistrust, or inequality? Pay attention to your feelings if you want to know whether or not you're on track. Positive emotions tell you that you're in harmony with your objectives; unpleasant emotions signal that you're out of alignment with your true purpose.

Your ideal magical partner is someone you can trust, enjoy, and feel comfortable with. It also helps if you find this person so incredibly attractive you get hot every time you think about him or her. When you work magic together, your feelings for one another enhance or detract from the spell or ritual. Some magicians can set aside their personal stuff and perceive whomever they're working with as a representation of the God or Goddess. Others can't.

According to some sources, your magic partner shouldn't be your spouse or significant other (although that might be tricky to work out with your spouse or significant other). Instead, your partner should be someone whose energy complements and elevates your own. We've all met people who turned us on, people with whom we had incredible sex, even though we didn't want to be in a long-term relationship with them. However, chemistry isn't the only determining factor. Often "chemistry" arises from unresolved Freudian-type mommy or daddy issues, projection, power plays, kinks, and other conditions that aren't particularly conducive to successful sex magic.

Some magicians recommend choosing a partner based on astrological considerations. Being an astrologer myself, I can see the validity in this. Don't just look at your sun signs, though—do a thorough synastry chart analysis to get the big picture. Venus and Mars connections can be more important than your sun positions. Other magicians suggest finding a partner to whom you're karmically connected. This, too, might be valid, though a bit harder to evaluate. Ostensibly, you have karmic connections with everyone who plays a significant role in your life—what type of karma do you want to bring to the bed?

As you can see, there's a lot of debate about the subject. Personally, I believe the most powerful sex magic blends love with passion, and doing magic with someone you love is usually preferable to working with someone for whom you only feel physical desire. Love enriches everything it touches. As the French mystic and philosopher Pierre Teilhard de Chardin wrote in *The Phenomenon of Man*, "Love alone is capable of uniting living beings in such a way as to complete and fulfill them, for it alone takes them and joins them by what is deepest in themselves."

Magician, Know Thyself

Before you start working with a partner, you may want to spend some time doing solo sex magic. Monofocal sex (meaning excitation, energy, and intention focused through a single magician, usually via masturbation) allows you to explore your sensual responses, increase your energy, and develop control at your own pace. You can relax, without fear of someone else's judgment. You become more comfortable with yourself and more accepting.

As Margo Anand explains in *The Art of Sexual Ecstasy,* "The more self-accepting you are, the more orgasmic you can become … When you criticize yourself, one part of you is fighting another part, and consequently your energy is in conflict. In a state of self-acceptance, your energy is unified." When you're conflicted, your ability to attract what you desire diminishes. When you're in harmony with yourself, you magnetize other people to you because you embody the serenity of self-acceptance that we all seek.

Women, in particular, can tend to be more concerned about pleasing their partners than with pleasing themselves. Or, we may place responsibility for our sexual satisfaction on our partners. By practicing solo sex, you learn to connect with the pleasure and power that are your nature, rather than looking for them outside yourself.

Working solo also reduces the possibility of conflicting objectives. You don't have to worry about whether your partner's telos is in agreement with yours, or if his/her emotions and yours are in the same place. You can do your own thing, and do it your way.

One Partner or Many?

Magic is synergistic. The sum is greater than the parts. Therefore, when you work with another person or a group who all have the same intention, the energy you raise and your power to produce an outcome become multiplicatively greater. And, of course, sex, like traveling, can be more fun if you share the experience with someone else.

The Advantages of Magical Monogamy

Once you've found a magical partner whom you've determined is right for you, it's often a good idea to continue working with that person on a regular basis rather than jumping around from partner to partner. Magic, like love, requires trust and commitment. Although you needn't be madly in love with your partner to do sex magic effectively, you do need to establish trust and commitment.

Over time, you'll also learn how to maximize your energy, generate the greatest amount of pleasure, and hone your focusing ability together. It's a bit like dancing—when you practice a lot with the same partner, a sort of intuition develops. You learn to move gracefully together and avoid stepping on one another's toes. If you keep changing partners, you'll have to start all over again with each new person.

The Value of Variety

On the other hand, you can learn different things from different people. You may even discover that certain pairings work best in certain instances—just as some wines pair better with some foods than others. You may be able to accomplish particular objectives with one partner and others with another person. A young, energetic lover might be an advantage if you're doing a rigorous or vigorous ritual, whereas a more mature, experienced lover could bring greater wisdom, control, and depth to a spell. Some spells or rituals may also benefit from specific energetic/astrological/karmic combinations.

Certain things can only be accomplished in certain kinds of pairings. For instance, you need a man and a woman to create what's sometimes called "elixir," a magically charged blend of male and female sexual fluids. (We'll talk more about this later.) If you and your primary magic partner are of the same gender, obviously you'll have to find someone of the opposite sex to work with if you intend to include elixir in a spell.

Group Sex Magic

If you're comfortable with the idea of group sex—and have found a group of like-minded individuals with whom you want to work—you can combine your energies and increase your magical power exponentially. However, group sex magic is *not* an orgy. It is a ritual that utilizes the combined sexual energies of the participants for a predetermined purpose.

Group sex magic can be performed in a number of ways. One form is actually a variation of monofocal sex that involves additional people. In this type of ritual, energy and intent are focused through one person—the primary magician—who is aroused and pleasured by other members of the group. These "assistants" may or may not arouse themselves, depending on what the group decides, but their main job is to bring the primary magician to the heights of excitation and exaltation.

In another version, the assistants engage in sex with each other, but the energy they raise and the group's telos are focused through the primary magician. Just as a healer might send energy toward another person, the assisting magicians use their thoughts and emotions to send their own sexual energy to the primary magician. The same "assisted loving" practices may be directed through a couple instead of an individual, in which case the assisting magicians channel their energy and intent through the designated couple.

In polyfocal sex magic, a group of magicians all engage in sex together. Each individual receives energy from the group into his/her body and transmits his/her own energy back to the group. This interaction can tremendously amplify the power in the ritual, as everyone is charging everyone else's batteries simultaneously. The trick is to stay focused, which isn't always easy when many people are involved—especially if those people aren't experienced magicians. For that reason, one magician often serves as a guide or facilitator for the group. Usually, this person doesn't participate in the sexual activity, but instead directs the energy raised by the group in much the same way as a conductor directs an orchestra or a quarterback leads a team.

I guess this is as good a place as any to mention "safe sex." But mention it is all I intend to do. After a quarter-century of information dissemination, you already know why and how not to spread nasty diseases to your intimate partners. Obviously, the more people you're involved with, the more important this becomes. Good communication, mutual respect, and trust are basic ingredients in any relationship—magical, sexual, or otherwise.

Sex Positions and Their Purposes

In magic, changing sexual positions is more than just a way to bring variety into the bedroom. Different positions and actions actually support and enhance different intentions. For simplicity, I use the words man and woman here; however, same-sex couples can read the following as persons playing masculine or feminine roles during sex.

Missionary Position

In the so-called "missionary" position, the woman assumes the role of receiver, the man as the giver or activator. He places his intention within her; she nurtures it and gives it form. Both physically and symbolically, this position enables the man to be the more active and mobile partner, to guide their movements and pace the act, and to generally take charge.

A couple chooses a "male superior" position to attract something the man desires. They perform the magic for his benefit. Perhaps he wants to get a job or improve his finances. Or, he might seek to heal a physical ailment. Both people agree to direct their thoughts, emotions, and sexual energy toward manifesting his objective.

Cowgirl Position

In what's sometimes called "cowgirl" style sex, the woman is on top, facing and straddling or "riding" the man. Here, the woman becomes the giver or initiator, while the man takes on the role of receiver. As the more active and mobile partner, she guides and paces their movements. She's in control.

A couple chooses a "female superior" position to attract something she desires—money, career success, good health, et cetera. The magic they do benefits her. Both people agree to direct their thoughts, emotions, and sexual energy toward manifesting her objective.

Doggie Style Position

In the so-called "doggie style" position, the man assumes the giver/activator role and the woman the role of recipient. He's on top, so again, he's the one with the greater degree of mobility and control. He's the master of this ceremony. He gets to direct the show and decide how the magic will be utilized.

Positions in which the participants do not face each other are used to send magic to someone else. Therefore, this position lets the man project energy to another person of his choosing. Perhaps he intends to heal a sick relative. Or, he wants to help a friend win a tennis match, get a promotion at work, or find a lover. The couple agrees to direct their thoughts, emotions, and sexual energy toward manifesting his objective.

Reverse Cowgirl Position

Here the woman is on top, straddling the man and facing away from him. And because she's on top, it's lady's choice. She has superior mobility and control, so she's the initiator and facilitator. She's physically and symbolically in charge.

This position enables the woman to send magical energy to someone of her choosing—a friend, relative, or even a complete stranger. Whatever her intention, the couple agrees to direct their thoughts, emotions, and sexual energy toward manifesting it.

Lotus Position

For people who feel comfortable sitting in this cross-legged position, with the woman seated on the man's lap, the lotus combines plenty of close, face-to-face, affectionate body contact, like the missionary position, with the female-in-charge qualities of the cowgirl. Because she's on top and has the greater degree of mobility, the couple chooses it to attract something the woman seeks. This is also a good position to use in conjunction with kundalini yoga breathing practices that enhance your ability to circulate energy through your bodies during sex.

Oral Sex

As with positions involving intercourse, oral sex magic acts can raise energy to support specific intentions for the people involved. In this case, however, the active partner gives the passive partner what s/he desires—sexually as well as magically—and helps to fulfill the recipient's objective. The person in control consciously cooperates in bringing about the passive person's goal. As I interpret this, lending your efforts and energy to further another's purpose is an act of generosity and devotion—but logistically it may also have something to do with the fact that the giver's head is ostensibly below the recipient's, and therefore in a "support" position. So if anyone has thoughts about this I'd be interested in hearing them.

A man may perform cunnilingus on a woman for the purpose of producing an outcome she wants. A woman may perform fellatio on a man to assist him in achieving something he desires. Engaging in mutual oral sex, what's sometimes referred to as 69, involves both giving and receiving simultaneously. Both people benefit. When your intent is to achieve a joint/mutual goal or to attract something you both want (such as a house you'll share), this practice lets you tap and blend your sexual energies simultaneously and direct them toward an agreed-upon goal.

Of course, you can do sex magic to fulfill the objectives of either partner—or both—using whatever position(s), method(s), or combinations you prefer. If you're really concerned about keeping things equal, lying side by side may be the best answer.

Three-Ways and Other Combinations

The more people you include in a sex act, the more complex the whole situation becomes. That doesn't mean it's a bad thing. As we just discussed, sex acts that blend the energies of several people can potentially generate more power than acts that engage two people only. In order to achieve the outcome you desire, however, everyone involved must agree on the intention and stay focused on the same goal.

Using the general descriptions above, you can design combinations to serve whatever purpose you choose. Let's say, for example, you want to set up a three-way pattern to help a man to get a new job. The job-seeker assumes the role of recipient; a female magician performs oral sex on him while another man penetrates her doggie style. In this arrangement, the man in the active position sends energy through the woman, who nurtures it and offers it to the job-seeker to support him in his employment search. Of course, this configuration can work with a same-sex threesome or other trio, too.

Any number of magicians can participate in a variety of arrangements, depending on your objectives and the people involved. You might even decide to invite nonphysical entities to join you (read on).

You'll find many variations of the positions discussed here. Some positions are designed to accommodate people with diminished flexibility or strength, or to provide greater comfort for partners of different sizes and shapes. These positions may modify or combine features of the basic positions previously mentioned. For example, spooning with the man behind and the woman facing away from him is a "sending" position, but somewhat more egalitarian than either doggie style or reverse cowgirl because neither partner is "superior." This could be a good one to use if you want to send energy to a mutual friend or relative. The *Kama Sutra* presents many options you might wish to try, and wiser magicians than I probably know the benefits of each position. Experiment and discover what works best for you.

Your intention, backed by genuine emotion, is more important than outer trappings. The suggestions offered here just help you fine-tune your efforts, perhaps by making you more physically aware of your telos.

Honesty Is Probably the Best Policy

Perhaps you fear your mate wouldn't approve, or would think you're weird, if you revealed your interest in sex magic. But you still want to make use of this awesome power. Do you have to tell your partner you're doing magic when you have sex?

The simple answer is no. You can raise sexual energy and fuel your intentions with it regardless of whether your partner knows what you're doing. You can secretly draw upon your partner's sexual energy to fuel your personal goals. However, openly sharing this experience with someone you're intimate with can strengthen your personal relationship, while also strengthening your spell.

From a practical standpoint, a partner who doesn't know your intentions may be feeling or thinking about something else at the key moment—and that could interfere with your objective. Only you can decide whether or not to reveal yourself to your partner. But if you don't feel comfortable enough with your mate to share something so important, you might consider finding another person with whom to engage in sex magic—even if that relationship doesn't extend beyond this circumscribed role. As an alternative, you could engage in solo sex magic or invite a nonphysical entity to be your partner.

Nonphysical Partners

Want to have sex with a god or goddess? It's possible, although invoking a spirit can be a tad more complex than picking up someone at the local singles' bar. The process can raise some pretty powerful energies, perhaps unlike anything you've experienced before, which may rock your world or be a bit unsettling.

The good news is, you're not likely to contract any STDs. The bad news is, there's always a risk of attracting an entity who has an agenda of its own, maybe an agenda you'd rather not be an accessory to. As a result, many magicians don't recommend this practice to beginners. I'm not going to tell you to avoid sex with spirits—that decision is yours to make. It's certainly nothing new, and some well-respected individuals, including the English poet William Blake, have written about it.

Invoking and Evoking Spirits

Invoking means drawing the powers of a nonphysical entity into yourself. You invite a spirit being to fill you with its qualities, characteristics, or abilities for a specified time and/or purpose. Perhaps you've heard the term "drawing down the moon." It refers to invoking a goddess into your body. "Drawing down the sun" means invoking a god. Magicians often do this when they perform "the Great Rite" (described in chapter 12).

Evoking means causing a nonphysical entity to appear in the physical world. You may actually see this being— perhaps as smoke or light—or merely sense its presence. You've undoubtedly heard of séances being conducted for this purpose. When you're evoking spirits, it's wise to remember an old saying among magicians: don't raise anything you can't put down. Calling up a powerful entity you can't control could lead to all sorts of tricky and uncomfortable situations.

Sex with Spirits

An *incubus* is a nonphysical masculine entity with whom you engage in sex. The feminine counterpart is known as a *succubus.*

As in the material world, there are good guys and bad guys in the spirit realm. If you opt to work with a nonphysical lover or to allow an entity into your body, it's best to choose a god, goddess, or angelic being—not one of the lower spirits. Yes, I know there's a current fascination with vampires, but giving one of those dudes access to your body—even if he does look like Johnny Depp—probably isn't a good idea.

To attract a spirit lover, begin by doing the usual clearing and banishing rituals. (See chapter 12 for instructions if you're not familiar with this.) If you wish, bring into your sacred space a picture, figurine, or other image of the entity you intend to attract. Arouse yourself sexually, using whatever method you prefer. Look at the image or envision the entity in your mind's eye.

Call to the deity you wish to attract and invite him/her to be your lover. Imagine him or her caressing you with the most exquisite touch, kissing and licking your body, doing anything and everything you desire to heighten your excitement. If you're working with an incubus, feel him plunge deep inside you. If you're working with a succubus, sense her heat and wetness surrounding your penis. Although traditionally, the deity assumes the "superior" position and active role while you enjoy being the recipient, you may choose to caress, kiss, and otherwise pleasure the nonphysical entity just as you would a physical partner.

Feel your energy and the deity's energy merge, dissolving into one another. Unlike having sex a physical partner, there are no flesh-and-blood boundaries separating you and your nonphysical lover. Receive the deity's energy through your genitals and let it flow into the rest of your body. Continue absorbing this energy, allowing it to expand and undulate through your body and mind, until you feel you've taken in all you possible can. When you're ready, orgasm as you send out your intention into the cosmic matrix.

Finish by thanking your partner. Then perform a banishing ritual to release any other beings or energies that might have been attracted by your spell.

Deities and Their Areas of Influence

When you call upon a god or goddess to assist you, consider selecting one who represents your intentions. For instance, Brigid is the Celtic goddess of poetry and smithcraft, so if you're trying to get a publisher to buy your latest collection of poems, Brigid would be a good deity to contact. Perhaps Mars could help you win an upcoming football game. Or, summon a deity to whom you feel a strong connection, such as one who's revered in your cultural/ethnic heritage or spiritual path.

Following you'll find a list of some well-known gods and goddesses and their areas of influence to help you determine which one(s) might best assist you. I suggest you do additional research, however, to learn more about these and other deities before you work with one. (In chapter 12 you'll find more instructions for contacting and invoking deities.)

Goddesses

Amaterasu (Japanese): beauty, leadership, brightness

Aphrodite (Greek): love, beauty, sensuality

Artemis (Greek): courage, independence, protection

Bast (Egyptian): playfulness, joy

Brigid (Celtic): creativity, smithcraft, inspiration, healing

Ceres (Roman): nourishment, health

Ceridwin (Celtic): inspiration, wisdom

Cybele (Asia Minor): fertility

Freya (Norse): love, healing, sensuality

Hathor (Egyptian): love

Isis (Egyptian): art, nourishment, wholeness, awakening

Kuan Yin (Chinese): compassion, humanitarianism, mercy

Lakshmi (Indian): wealth, abundance

Sekmet (Egyptian): grace, dignity, strength

Sophia (Greek): wisdom, primal power

Tara (Indian): nourishment, protection, compassion

Yemaja (Nigerian): secrets, dreams, childbirth, purification

Gods

Aengus (Irish): youth, love

Ahura Mazda (Persian): knowledge

Apollo (Greek): beauty, poetry, music, healing

Ganesh (Indian): strength, perseverance, overcoming obstacles

Green Man (Celtic): fertility, nature, abundance, sexuality

Horus (Egyptian): knowledge, eternal life, protection

Lugh (Celtic): craftsmanship, healing

Mars (Roman): aggression, war, vitality, courage

Mercury (Roman): intelligence, communication, trade, travel

Mithras (Persian): strength, virility, courage

Odin/Woden (Scandinavian): knowledge, poetry, prophesy

Osiris (Egyptian): cultivation, civilization, learning

Thoth (Egyptian): knowledge, science, the arts

Tyr (Teutonic): law, athletics

Zeus (Greek): authority, justice, abundance, magnanimity

(Lists excerpted from *The Everything Wicca and Witchcraft Book* by Skye Alexander, published by Adams Media 2008)

What About Kinky Stuff?

It's been said that erotica is something you find enticing, whereas pornography is something another person finds enticing and you find disgusting. The same applies to kinky. "Kinky" is in the eye of the beholder. Furthermore, our ideas about such things change over time. Let's face it, a lot of people would consider sex magic pretty kinky. And even by today's standards, most folks would call Crowley one kinky dude (an image he encouraged).

Personally, I believe whatever consenting adults want to do with one another is their business. Having said that, I urge you to pay attention to your emotions with regard to any particular sex act, partner, or situation. Your emotions will tell you whether it's right or wrong *for you*. If you don't feel comfortable, don't do it—you could be creating something you don't really want.

All emotions—positive and negative—produce results. Therefore, it's best to seek experiences that elevate your resonance, joy, and personal power. As we've said before, you can only draw good things to you when you feel good. Sex that makes you feel good about yourself increases your ability to attract abundance and happiness into your life. Sexual practices that cause pain, humiliation, degradation, fear, or other feelings that don't support your sense of yourself as a valuable being will weaken your resonance and call up circumstances that further undermine you.

seven

Maximizing
Sexual Energy

It's often said that the mind is the most sensitive erogenous zone. When doing sex magic, you want to stimulate
and tantalize your mind to the nth degree. Because your
thoughts and emotions attract your life circumstances,
spend some time each day training your mind in the fine
art of fantasizing. Indulge your imagination. Mentally
explore a wide range of sexual possibilities, things you'd
like to do with your partner and things you think might
be fun to experiment with and explore. Picture yourself
engaging in activities you've never tried before, that may lie
a little bit outside your range of familiarity. Joshua Geller,
writing on www.spiritual.com.au, suggests that breaking

through inhibitions and barriers can be a powerful formula in sex magic.

If you like, read erotic literature. I recommend reading rather than watching X-rated movies because reading trains your imagination. It requires you to create mental pictures of what's going on instead of passively observing the action playing out before you on a TV screen. Better yet, try your hand at writing erotica. As we've already discussed, visualization is a key ingredient in magical work, and writing is a potent form of magic.

Tell your lover what you'd like to do, or talk about what you're going to do—both before and during sex. Write him a really juicy letter (texting just isn't quite the same). Leave a hot message on her voice mail. Try phone sex. One of my friends used to enjoy making love with one man while another "talked dirty" to her on the phone. Do whatever sparks your imagination and kindles your inner fire.

Let time be your ally—not only during the act itself, but beforehand as well. A lover and I used to plan our sex magic rituals well in advance, not only because it took a while to organize all the details, but because the anticipation added to our excitement. If he was designing the ritual, he'd call me every day for a week and ask me to collect one thing we'd need—a certain type of candle, for example, or a particular herb. Of course, the entire time I was shopping for the candle or hunting in the woods for the special herb, I kept thinking about him and what we'd do when we finally got together. It was a whole week of foreplay!

Energy-Sensing Exercises

Magic involves mentally manipulating energy to manifest the outcomes you choose. Before you can do that, however, you need to become aware of your own energy and the energy patterns around you. Try these simple exercises, which let you sense the energy that surrounds and permeates your body, the energy that animates you and all life forms, what the Chinese call *chi*. The more sensitive you are to these energies, the better you'll be at controlling them to produce outcomes.

Exercise #1

Hold your hands up and open in front of you, about a foot apart with your palms facing. Slowly move your hands closer together until you feel a slight pressure, as if you were holding something between them very lightly. Perhaps you'll experience warmth, tingling, tickling, an airy sensation like a faint breeze brushing your palms, or something else. Most people notice this when their hands are a few inches apart, and the feeling gets stronger as the distance between the palms decreases. What you are sensing is your aura.

Now, rub your palms together briskly for a few moments, until they feel warm. Again, hold them facing each other. Is the sensation stronger?

Exercise #2

Next, try working with a partner. Stand or sit facing one another. Both of you hold your hands up and open in front of you, so that your palms face your partner's. You should leave about a foot of space between your hands and your partner's hands. Slowly move your palms closer to your partner's until you feel a sensation similar to what you experienced when you did the exercise alone. As you close the gap between your hands, the sensation will intensify. What you're sensing now is your partner's aura touching your own.

Exercise #3

Sit in a chair and ask your partner to stand behind you. Close your eyes. Your partner holds his/her hands several inches above the crown of your head, palms open and turned toward your head. Slowly, your partner draws his/her hands down the sides of your head toward your shoulders, without actually touching you. Do you feel a tingling or tickling sensation? Something else?

Switch places. See what your partner experiences when you brush his/her aura with your hands.

Exercise #4

Lie on your back on the bed or floor and close your eyes. Ask your partner to hold his/her open palms a few inches above your head, and then slowly run them down along the length of your body—without actually touching you. What do you feel? Do you sense different things in different parts of your body? Is the sensation stronger or weaker in certain places?

Turn over on your stomach and ask your partner to repeat the aura-stroking process. What do you feel now?

Switch roles and stroke your partner's aura. Discuss your experiences.

Exercise #5

Stand or sit with your eyes closed. Ask your partner to stare at a place on your body and focus attention there. He or she should imagine sending energy, like a beam of light, toward you. Relax and let yourself feel your partner's eyes on you—don't think about it or try to guess where your partner might be staring. You may notice a tingling, tickling, or warmth in a particular spot. With your finger, point to the place where you feel his/her attention. Open your eyes. Did you correctly identify the spot?

Switch roles. Now direct your attention to a particular place on your partner's body. Send a focused ray of energy, like a beam of light, toward your partner. Ask your partner to point to the place where s/he feels your attention. Is s/he correct?

Seeing Auras

Most people's auras extend several inches to a foot or more out from their bodies. However, you can expand your aura with a little practice, through breath work, visualization, yoga, and other techniques. Your aura usually expands during sex, too.

You may be able to see people's auras. Often an aura appears as a faint, whitish glow like a halo around the person's head and/or outlining the body. If you're especially sensitive, you might notice colors in someone's aura. It's usually easier to see an aura if the person stands in front of a dark background.

You might also try observing your own aura. Hold your hand a few inches above a dark cloth. Do you see a slight halo around your hand or a pale haze extending from your fingertips? Slowly move your hand. Do you notice faint whitish trails following the movement of your hand?

Practice until you feel capable of sensing, sending, and receiving energy easily. You'll use this technique frequently when doing magic. Energy can even be transmitted over great distances. Wherever thought goes, energy flows.

Common-Sense Ways to Raise Your Energy Level

The more vitality you have, and the stronger your personal vibration is, the faster you'll attract what you desire. The more vitality you have, the more you can enjoy sex, too. All energy—physical, emotional, and psychic—is connected; you can't separate one from the other. Holistic healers, and even many conventional allopathic doctors, accept that your thoughts and feelings influence your physical condition and well-being. Likewise, your physical health can affect your emotions. Therefore, it makes sense to nurture yourself in all ways, so your energy level stays high enough to manifest your intentions successfully. You've heard the following advice again and again—now consider it in the context of sex and magic.

Exercise

You don't need to hire a personal trainer or sign up for civilian boot camp. Do something you enjoy, that makes you feel good. Take regular walks in nature. Ride your bike. Dance. Do yoga. Before each workout or activity, state your intention to improve your health, happiness, and overall well-being by engaging in this activity or workout. Exercise can improve sex, too. If you're in good physical shape, you'll be able to make love longer and with greater gusto—you might even master some of those challenging positions in the *Kama Sutra*.

Eat Right

Everybody's different, and there's no such thing as a "one size fits all" diet. Vegan fare might suit some people; others may function better when they eat plenty of meat and protein. Few of us, however, thrive on a diet of donuts, sodas, and fast-food burgers. Magic emphasizes mind over matter, but if sugar and food additives bounce your brain chemistry around like a basketball, your magical power could be impaired.

A healthy diet can improve sex, too. Intercourse is easier if you don't have to maneuver around a big belly. Additionally, when you feel good about the way you look, your sexual pleasure and your power of attraction soar.

Get Enough Sleep

Sleep deprivation has been used as a form of torture. Lack of sleep diminishes your vitality and your ability to think clearly, and by extension your effectiveness as a magician. When you sleep better you feel better, and when you feel better your magical power increases.

Adequate sleep can improve sex, too. About 25 percent of people who participated in a National Sleep Foundation survey in 2005 said their intimate relationships were damaged because they were too tired for sex.

Limit Consumption of Alcohol and Other Drugs

Although mind-altering substances play a role in some magic rituals and ceremonies, ingesting alcohol or other drugs affects your thinking, emotions, and physical abilities. When you're doing magic, it's usually best to keep a clear head. Limiting your consumption of alcohol and other drugs can improve sex, too. A drink before sex can relax your inhibitions and get you in the mood—but overindulge and you might not make it to the grand finale.

Meditate

Hundreds of clinical studies have demonstrated meditation's ability to facilitate relaxation and promote mind-body harmony. Meditation helps you clear and focus your mind. It balances your emotions. By reducing stress, it enables you to stop wasting energy.

Meditation can improve sex, too. In the section titled "Awakening Chakra Energy" later in this chapter, you'll find a meditation/visualization technique to enhance your sexual energy.

Unlocking Your Sexual Energy

Many of us settle for only a fraction of the pleasure we could enjoy. The difference between ordinary sex and "ecstatic sex" is like the difference between fast food and a gourmet meal. In ordinary sex, orgasm is localized in the genital area. In ecstatic sex, your orgasm flows in an undulating, wavelike motion through your entire body and brain. In ordinary sex, tension builds rapidly to a brief climax and quickly diminishes. In ecstatic sex, you remain in a high state of arousal for an extended period of time, balancing excitation with relaxation; orgasm lasts much longer and may lead to an altered state of consciousness. Instead of feeling drained afterwards, you feel enlivened and empowered.

Tension Inhibits Sensation

To experience ecstasy, you have to relax. When your muscles tighten, in response to anger, fear, stress, or other painful emotions, energy stops flowing smoothly in your body. Over time, these emotions get bound up in the muscles and cannot be expressed naturally or released. Trapped energy, like a clogged stream, begins to stagnate. Scientist Wilhelm Reich wrote about the results of chronic muscular tension, which he called "body armoring," in *The Function of the Orgasm*, *The Cancer Biopathy*, and other books. According to Reich, body armoring prevented adequate sexual functioning, which led to the development of cancer and other diseases.

Think of your body as a container for sexual energy. When your muscles are relaxed, your "container" becomes more flexible and can expand to allow for the buildup of energy. Muscle tension—which can exist even if your muscles seem slack or layers of fat cover them—makes it difficult for your body to hold a sexual charge. The result may be premature ejaculation, an inability to reach a high level of excitation, or another form of sexual dysfunction. The Tibetan Buddhist teacher Lama Yeshe called the sexual force the "raw oil of the body." When you're relaxed and free of blockages, sexual energy can oil the intricate machinery of your body so that it functions optimally.

Therapeutic Touch

Massage can help relax your muscles and facilitate the flow of energy through your body. Sharing a sensual massage with a partner can be a delicious prelude to sex, too. Bring your olfactory sense into play by blending an enticing essential oil into your favorite massage oil or lotion. (You'll find a list of suggested aromas in chapter 9.) Note that some essential oils can be irritating to skin, so you may want to avoid massaging your nipples or sex organs with these.

Reflexology involves rubbing places on your feet (and sometimes hands) to stimulate energy and heal conditions in other areas of your body. The right foot corresponds to the right side of the body—the left foot to the left side. The part from your arch to your toes corresponds to the upper half of your body; from the arch to the heel relates to the lower half of your body. To relieve tension in your stomach or abdomen, which can block sexual feelings, massage your arches. Massaging the top of your foot where it joins the ankle can enhance your libido. Rub the points on the outer part of the foot below the ankle bone near the heel to aid impotence. For women, pressing the center of the heel on the sole of the foot can help alleviate sexual problems, too.

Acupuncture and acupressure also remove blockages in the body's energy channels (called meridians). On the lower back, on either side of the spine in the sacral bone area, you'll find what are known as the sacral points. Pressing these points firmly with your thumbs or fingers for a minute or two can ease tension and stimulate the circulation of energy through the pelvic region. Also consider pressing two other points called the Sea of Vitality, located on the back at waist-level and about two finger-widths out from the spine, to balance the flow of sexual energy.

Awakening Chakra Energy

Breathing exercises, too, can relieve muscular tension and heighten vitality. Most of us tend to breathe shallowly, expanding only our chests when we inhale. Breathing slowly and deeply, allowing air to fill your stomach as well as your chest, calms stress and brings more life-giving oxygen into your body. During sex, deep breathing relaxes your muscles and postpones orgasm. It allows you to experience greater levels of excitation before orgasm and to enjoy a stronger, longer orgasm.

A school of yoga known as *kundalini,* a Sanskrit word that means "coiled up," utilizes breathing techniques to raise and direct energy. According to kundalini's practitioners, primal energy—sexual energy—resides at the base of the spine like a coiled serpent. Through special breathing and postures, you can awaken this powerful force and move it from its home in the root chakra (one of the body's seven major energy centers) up through the body to the top of the head. Along the way, this energy nourishes your entire system.

Chakra is a Sanskrit word that means "wheel." Eastern medicine tells us the body has seven major chakras aligned from the base of the spine to the top of the head. These energy centers influence us physically, emotionally, mentally, and spiritually. Although most people can't see them, they are vortices of light and portals through which the creative force of the universe enters our bodies. When the chakras become blocked or unbalanced due to stress, trauma, or illness, life energy gets stuck. Physical and/or emotional problems can occur as a result.

The Breath of Fire

A kundalini breathing technique called "Breath of Fire" or "Bellows Breath" gives you an immediate energy boost. It involves breathing through your nose with quick, short, snortlike breaths while you pump your stomach like a bellows. Take a deep breath to begin, and then exhale half the breath while you pull your stomach in. Inhale air quickly through your nose as you relax your stomach, and then exhale sharply through your nose as you pull your stomach in. Inhalations and exhalations should be of equal length, without pauses in between.

It takes a bit of concentration, but try to maintain a rhythmic pace for a minute or more if possible. This technique activates the sexual energy at the base of your spine and allows it to expand. By stimulating your life force, this breathing exercise enhances your sense of personal power, heightens your resonance, and relieves anxiety as well—all of which contribute to your sexual pleasure and magical ability.

Sex Energy Visualization

You can also mobilize sexual energy through visualization. Close your eyes and turn your attention to your root chakra at the base of your spine. Imagine your life force glowing there, like a bed of red-hot coals. Breathe slowly and deeply, drawing oxygen all the way down to this chakra—your breath causing the hot coals to ignite. Feel the pleasant heat at the base of your spine. As you mentally fan the flames, allow sexual feelings to awaken in your genitals.

Now, imagine the flames rising into your lower abdomen and your sacral chakra. The sacral chakra (another of the body's major energy centers), located about a hand's width below your belly button, is associated with sexuality. Let the sensual feelings you've ignited spread into your abdomen, stomach, hips, thighs, and elsewhere. Keep your mind focused on your inner fire as you turn up the heat and increase the pleasurable sensations. Enjoy these feelings for as long as you like. When you're ready, allow the fire to die down again to glowing embers at the base of your spine. You can awaken it again anytime you wish.

Open Your Heart

Ecstasy isn't merely a genital affair. Ecstasy is a total body-mind-spirit experience, and to achieve it you have to open your heart. The energy center known as the heart chakra, located in the center of your chest near your physical heart, marks the halfway point between the lower and the upper chakras. Some metaphysicians teach that the physical heart not only serves as a pump to move blood through your body, it regulates and balances your complete energy system. A closed heart blocks the flow of energy between the upper and lower parts of your body. It limits your ability to experience joy, health, and well-being. Patients with coronary problems "are people who only want to listen to their heads, and in whose lives the heart figures far too little," write Thorwald Dethlefsen and Rudiger Dahlke, M.D. in their book *The Healing Power of Illness*. "Only a hard heart can break!"

Here's a simple exercise that can help open your heart chakra and facilitate the movement of vital energy through your body. Stand and clasp your hands behind you, keeping your arms straight so that your hands rest near your tailbone (the root chakra). Pull your shoulders back as far as you can comfortably, as if trying to get your shoulder blades to touch. Lift your chin slightly. Feel the stretch across your chest. Slowly raise your arms, keeping your hands clasped and your arms straight, until your arms are parallel to the floor (at a 90-degree angle to your torso, or as close to this as you can get). As you lift your arms, imagine your heart opening wide, like a flower blossoming.

Hold this position for thirty seconds or longer, while you breathe as deeply as possible and expand your chest. Feel your emotional barriers crumbling as the healing power of love radiates in your heart center. Then release the posture and shake your arms. Repeat a few times. Afterwards, you may feel a greater sense of compassion, acceptance, expansiveness, rejuvenation, or something else.

Many good books have been written about the chakras. You may wish to increase your understanding of these energy centers, so you can work more successfully with your own vital energy and with the animating force of the universe.

Increasing Sexual Power

Tantra teaches breathing practices you can do with a partner to heighten your sexual energy. "Tantra is a cult of ecstasy," Kamala Devi writes in *The Eastern Way of Love*. "Sex is holy to a Tantric… it is energizing and life-giving."

Body Talk

Here's a technique that cycles energy through your bodies, harmonizing and increasing your power. Choose a sexual position that involves genital contact, and determine which person will assume the active role. This person inhales through the nose and exhales through the genitals. Of course, you do this partly in your mind—you probably won't actually expel air through your genitals. The receptive partner does the opposite, inhaling through the genitals and exhaling through the nose. Again, some of this will be done through visualization. Focus your attention on your breathing. Allow your breathing to become synchronized, until the two of you are breathing together as one. Feel the energy cycling smoothly through your bodies and minds, expanding and intensifying with each breath. Continue for as long as you like.

Sex is a form of intimate communication between partners. Sex is the body's language, its native tongue. On *Rob's Magick Blog* (http://robjo.wordpress.com), Robert A. Peregrine writes, "sex can be used as a sort of courier … it can be used to transmit simple thoughts and emotions between two people. Or it can be used as a means to communicate information which cannot be communicated through typical means."

As you breathe together and move together, you erase the boundaries between you. You open yourselves to one another, and share not only physical intimacy, but emotional and spiritual intimacy as well. You communicate from the most essential part of your being. When you connect with a magical lover in this way, you can achieve wondrous things.

"Intent determines Sexual meaning, both to those with whom we engage and to ourselves," Nigris, O' writes in "An Essay on Sex and Sex Magic," published on www.spiritual .com.au. "When I am open, attracted and sincere, I have the most to give and to receive. Indeed, the most potentially moving experience within Sexuality derives from a willingness to interact honestly."

Slow Down to Build Power

Many of us learned at an early age to rush through sex. We didn't want our parents to catch us masturbating in the bathroom or the cops to catch us getting it on in the back seat of a parked car. *Psychology Today* reports that the average duration of foreplay is 15.4 minutes. And according to WebMD, a website that provides information from physicians around the world, the average length of time between penetration and ejaculation is 5.4 minutes. But "wham, bam, thank you ma'am" has no place in sex magic. Drawing out the experience and allowing your sexual energy to build gradually enhances your magical power.

Whether you're working with one partner, many, or alone, you can heighten your pleasure and your power of attraction by mastering the art of arousal. Take your time. Luxuriate in your sensuality. Let your excitement slowly increase until you feel almost ready to come. Then back off. Do some deep breathing. Shift from genital stimulation to stroking other parts of the body: arms, back, feet, and so on. When the immediacy has subsided, gradually elevate the level of excitation until, once again, you almost reach the point of no return. Ease off again. Continue this in the manner for as long as you like, slowly and steadily building intensity. With practice, you'll learn to "stay on the edge" for an extended period of time—you may even enter an altered state of consciousness.

During this period of high arousal, keep your telos in mind. The more intense your feelings, the faster you can attract what you desire, and in this near-orgasmic state your magnetic power is tremendous. You don't have to focus keenly on your objective all the time, but remain aware of your purpose for engaging in this sexual ritual. As you raise energy and cycle it through your body, mentally attach your intention to that energy.

Projecting Your Telos into the Matrix

When you're finally ready to release the energy you've built up, hold your telos clearly in your mind and feel the pleasure of having your desired outcome manifested in your life. Then let your orgasm wash through you. As it does, it sweeps your intention before it, like a wave pushing a boat along on its crest. The momentum you've generated carries your telos out into the universe, where it lodges in the fertile womb of the matrix and creates a magical child.

Chaos magicians, however, approach this in a slightly different way. Instead of focusing on a particular thought at the moment of orgasm, they attempt to empty their minds and allow the energy to move freely toward a goal that's been pre-established. You might want to experiment with both techniques.

Don't Stop at the Genitals

You can mentally direct the powerful orgasmic force upward from the genitals through the body's chakras and into the brain. Like water gushing through a pipe, the energy rises through a channel in the body, clearing away blockages in the various vortices and healing old emotional wounds. Your entire body may convulse uncontrollably and/or you might feel an intense emotional release. You might see an explosion of light, like fireworks inside your head, or sense yourself merging and melting into your partner. The experience may seem almost mystical.

"Orgasm is considered to be the moment when 'the gates of heaven open up'; for a while the barriers between the restricted physical world and the limitless heavens dissolve," Anja Heij writes on www.spiritual.com.au. "I feel a large amount of hot energy along my spine and the chakras in my head, while the crown chakra feels like a wide opened chalice or lotus flower."

After Orgasm

After orgasm, relax and stop thinking about your telos. Allow the universe to do its part now. Enjoy the calm after the tempest. Because your chakras have opened during sex, you may feel somewhat dazed or disoriented for a while. Take some time to regroup. Your energy and your partner's are still joined, so remain close together for a bit. Let your sexual fluids mingle with your partner's. Give your vagina or your penis a chance to absorb the energy of this magically charged blend. If you and your partner are of different genders, you can use this "elixir" in magical ways that we'll discuss later.

Many magicians recommend performing a banishing ritual after doing sex magic. (In chapter 12 you'll find instructions for banishing.) The energy you've raised can attract nonphysical entities you may not want to have hanging around, so when you've recovered, it's a good idea to send them on their way.

eight

Empowering
Your Intentions

In the previous chapter, you practiced working with your etheric energy body. Sometimes called your aura, this nonphysical body senses and reacts to anything that comes near to your physical body. Like a second skin, it responds to the touch of another person's energy body—even to another person's thoughts.

Although most of the time you probably don't pay much attention to your aura, it's on the job 24/7, gleaning information like an overzealous detective from everything in your environment. Likewise, other people's auras contin-ually pick up signals from you. Long before you exchange words with someone you meet, your auras have already communicated. Attraction or repulsion may result from this auric contact.

Your aura isn't static, however. It changes according to your thoughts and emotions. Your health and physical conditions also affect it. Psychics and other intuitive individuals often see shifts in your aura as colors rippling around your physical body like an aurora borealis. Furthermore, you can manipulate your energy field intentionally, expanding, contracting, or intensifying its resonance to produce an impact. Most likely, you've already done this many times, you just didn't realize it. Learning to consciously manipulate your energy is an important part of working magic.

As we've already discussed, the resonance of your energy field determines what you attract to you. The stronger, clearer, and more joyful your resonance, the greater your magnetic force. Feelings of unworthiness, doubt, desperation, or fear of disappointment block your ability to create what you desire. You can't attract big if you're feeling small. In *The Power of Intention,* Dr. Wayne W. Dyer reminds us, "We must always remember that nothing is disallowed by the universal mind. Whatever is not allowing us to be happy is being disallowed by us."

Connecting with the Earth

In just a moment, we're going to explore some techniques for manipulating your energy to produce the results you desire. But first you'll want to learn to draw upon the limitless creative power of the earth. This not only helps you stay grounded during the trance-like states that can occur when you do magic, it also nourishes your personal energy field so you don't burn out.

Developing a strong connection with the earth strengthens your magnetic force. The earth is our source of sustenance. She supplies us with the food we eat, the fuel we use to heat our homes and drive our cars, the materials from which we create our buildings, furnishings, clothing, and virtually everything else we require for survival. You can draw upon this fertile source of power to bolster your own creative ability and to make your dreams manifest in the material world.

Make Physical Contact with the Earth

One simple way to do this is to spend some time daily sitting or lying on the ground. Release all thoughts from your mind and focus your attention on the ground under you—the grass, soil, rocks, or whatever. (If you can't do this outdoors, sit on the floor and use your imagination to connect with the earth beneath the building.) Sense your body making a connection with Mother Earth. Allow yourself to relax. Feel her supporting and nourishing you. You might even hear the earth humming. Notice the vibration of her heartbeat, and experience her loving energy sustaining you.

Tap into the Earth's Energy

Here's another method you can use to draw upon the earth's vast energy resources. Stand with your eyes closed. Envision yourself sending a "taproot" down through the soles of your feet and deep into the center of the earth. Now, inhale slowly as you draw the earth's nurturing energy up through that taproot, into your body. Feel the energy rise through your chakras, along your spine, and spout out the top of your head, like a geyser. As you exhale, let this energy shower you with its radiance. Repeat this several times.

Become a Human Pentagram

If you prefer, you can become a human pentagram. The pentagram, after all, symbolizes the body's five "points": arms, legs, and head. It also represents the element of earth. Stand with your feet spread about shoulder-width apart and your arms outstretched parallel to the ground. Close your eyes and take a few moments to feel the solidity of the earth beneath you. As you inhale, imagine drawing energy up from the earth through the sole of your left foot to the top of your head. As you exhale, envision the energy running down through your body to your right foot and into the ground. Inhale again and pull energy up your right foot and leg, across your body to your left arm and hand. Exhale and feel the energy cross your chest to your right arm and hand. Inhale as you send the energy back down your left leg and foot, and into the earth.

Projecting the Energy of Attraction

When you pump yourself up for an important job interview, a big game, or a hot date, you manipulate your aura to achieve a particular objective. You infuse your energy field with your desire: to get the job, the trophy, the girl or guy. You project an energetic image of how you want others to see you—confident, powerful, dignified, sexy, mysterious, or whatever. Entertainers and politicians are experts at doing this. They've mastered the art of creating illusions that will elicit specific reactions from other people.

Want to make yourself more appealing? Forget about coloring your hair or bleaching your teeth. It's faster and cheaper to manipulate your energy field to attract whomever or whatever you desire. It's also more effective.

Engage Your Lust to Attract a Lover

Begin by connecting with the emotion of what you desire. If you seek a sex partner, for example, allow yourself to really engage your own lust. Fill yourself up with longing. Revel in it. Stoke those inner fires. Let your passion shimmer around you like heat waves rising off a West Texas highway on a summer day. Feel it ooze from your pores like the headiest perfume. Imagine the energy you've raised expanding and swirling around you, forming a seductively scented mist about a foot or two thick. Keep pushing your desire into your aura until it's so infused with sexy energy that anyone who comes within arm's reach of you will instantly get a jolt.

When you're hot and horny, turn your attention to your sacral chakra, the energy center located about a hand's width below your belly button. Eastern spiritual and healing traditions associate the sacral chakra with sexual feelings and the sex organs. Project your emotion out from this chakra, as if you were a lighthouse shining a light from your body to guide a lover to you. Thrust this highly charged energy outward, toward a specific person or into a whole room full of people. Keep radiating energy out from your sacral chakra, like the sun beaming through the solar system, heating up everyone in your presence. Before long, the target of your projection—or a number of people in the immediate vicinity—will respond to your energy.

One afternoon I strolled through Harvard Square in Cambridge, Massachusetts, after spending a couple steamy hours in bed with my lover. Everyone I passed turned to look at me. They reacted to the high-energy vibes I was resonating and felt drawn to me, even though they didn't know why.

Improve Your Image

You can use the same technique to serve other objectives, too. If you're trying to command respect on the playing field or in the boardroom, rev up feelings of confidence and invincibility, until your engine's roaring like a Boeing 747 preparing for takeoff. Ratchet up your emotions to the highest level you can achieve. The more intense and upbeat your feelings are, the greater your magnetic ability and the faster you'll get results. Then project those emotions through your solar plexus, the chakra associated with self-esteem and personal power. (This chakra is located about halfway between your heart and your belly button.) If your goal is to increase prosperity, focus energy through your root chakra, at the base of your spine. To attract love, project loving feelings from your heart chakra.

Projections of this sort are relatively short-lived, however. If you want to maintain a projection's attracting power, you have to nourish it. You need to continue infusing your aura with emotional energy that's consistent with your objective. In some instances, this happens naturally enough. Your passion for a person, an idea, or a situation keeps "feeding" the projection. If you've ever played sports, you've experienced the growing excitement and sense of power that circulate among members of a team during an important game. The players' enthusiasm nurtures the projection and maintains its strength. The fans' encouragement adds to the projection, which partly explains why teams tend to win more games at home than away.

Remember, your aura changes with your moods, and other people sense those changes. So, if you're meeting with someone you hope will finance a pet project you're working on and you notice feelings of inadequacy or anxiety creeping in, either consciously shift your emotions to a more positive level or take a break and resume the meeting at another time.

Amplifying Your Energy with Crystals

Quartz crystals hold, amplify, and transmit information. One of the most abundant and versatile minerals on earth, quartz is the main component of myriad precious, semiprecious, and commonplace stones. Many of the best crystals come from Madagascar and Brazil, but Arkansas is a rich source for quality stones, too. Some metaphysicians believe extraterrestrial beings brought crystals to our planet eons ago; others suggest crystals existed on the lost continents of Lemuria and Atlantis.

Regardless of their origins, crystals can be valuable assets in all kinds of spellcasting. You can use crystals (and other gemstones) to:

· Draw energy to you

· Project energy toward someone or something

· Contain energy

· Increase or enhance energy

· Accelerate action

These properties serve you well when you're working with projections, because a crystal can augment, focus, and help to sustain the projection. You don't have to do all the work yourself!

Clearing Your Crystal

Acquire a basic generator crystal of a size you can comfortably carry in your pocket. This common type of crystal usually has six faces that come together to form a point, and the base is flat so the crystal can stand upright. You can also wear a crystal—just make sure it hasn't been drilled for mounting as this kills the stone, leaving a lifeless shell.

Cleanse the crystal by holding it under running, tepid water for a few moments. Then clear it of all old programs, ideas, intentions, and other information that may have accumulated or been placed in the crystal prior to your acquisition of it. To do this, gently rub a piece of citrine along the sides of the crystal while simultaneously blowing on the crystal sharply. (If you don't have a piece of citrine, you can rub the crystal briskly with your thumb.) Do this for a minute or two, or until you sense you've removed any unwanted stuff.

If the crystal seems dull or unresponsive, it could be asleep, in which case you'll have to work with it for a while to awaken its power. Hold it, meditate with it, talk to it, send it loving thoughts, and build a connection with the stone.

Programming Your Crystal

Now your crystal is ready to receive your intention. Hold the crystal while you create your projection, as we discussed previously. When your resonance is at its peak—when you feel hot and horny, superconfident, or all charged up—attach your intention to this energy. Then mentally send it into the crystal. For instance, you could hold the crystal to your "third eye" and imagine a ray of light entering the crystal, then fanning out from the crystal as the energy flows into your environment. You might even feel the stone tingling or becoming warmer, or see it sparkle in response. Carry the crystal on your person to amplify and sustain the power of your projection.

Although you can use a clear quartz crystal for any intention, certain stones possess natural qualities of their own that may enhance and support your objective. Consider working with these stones for specific purposes:

- *Love:* rose quartz

- *Sex/passion:* carnelian

- *Relationship issues:* tangerine quartz

- *Prosperity:* abundance crystal (one with greenish traces of chlorite in it)

- *Insight/intuition:* sapphire

- *Communication/intellect:* aquamarine

- *Peace/relaxation:* amethyst

- *Confidence:* topaz

· *Courage/strength:* ruby

· *Protection:* clear quartz

We'll talk more about crystals and gemstones later. You'll also find many good books about crystals that explain how to work with them for healing, attraction, protection, and more.

Casting a Glamour

Remember the refrain from *Snow White:* "Mirror, mirror on the wall. Who's the fairest of them all?" When you're casting a glamour, the answer is *you.*

In magic, the term "glamour" refers to a type of energy manipulation that causes other people to see you the way you want to be seen. You can make yourself appear more attractive, formidable, intelligent, successful, or anything else you desire. Just as you might wear a particular outfit to present a certain image, you magically don a glamour for the same reason. Basically, a glamour is an illusion—a trick that fools the eye, like a *trompe l'oeil* painting. You don't actually change yourself, you merely project a mirage around you that temporarily alters other people's perceptions of you.

Smoke and Mirrors

When you cast a glamour, you don't focus on any specific feature that you wish looked different. For instance, if you think your thighs are too fat, don't try to visualize them thinner—you'll merely draw attention to your thighs. And don't try to create a precise image of beauty, strength, or intelligence—you'll limit yourself and your possibilities.

Beauty (or strength or success) is in the eye of the beholder. What appeals to one person might turn off someone else. Instead, you'll get better results if you tap into the essence of what you seek to be and let other people fill in the details that appeal to them. That may sound a bit vague, but we're dealing with smoke and mirrors here.

Let's say you want people to perceive you as beautiful. We all know men and women who aren't especially good-looking, yet they never lack admirers. There's something attractive about them. In many cases, it's because they feel good about themselves. They think they're desirable, and therefore other people do, too. Their belief in their own value boosts their resonance and makes them shine. A glamour is a bit more manipulative and not as genuine as a true sense of self-worth. Still, a successful glamour relies on your ability to convince yourself—and others—that you are, indeed, beautiful, although you don't look even remotely like a *Vogue* supermodel.

Indulge Your Vanity

Start by gazing at yourself in a mirror, naked. A full-length one that enables you to see your whole body is ideal. (I have a six-foot-tall mirror with an ornately carved frame that lets me pretend I'm the equivalent of Botticelli's *Venus*.) Many of us, when we view ourselves in the mirror, tend to focus on all those little "imperfections," but to cast a glamour you must first find something about yourself that you consider attractive. Everyone has a least one beautiful aspect. As you focus on that feature, indulge your vanity. Silence the inner judge and listen to the pep squad. Praise yourself and enjoy how that feels. (If you could see your aura, you'd notice it just brightened a bit.)

Now take this narcissism a step further. Talk to yourself. Don't just compliment the feature you initially decided was attractive, expand your self-adoration to encompass all of you. Say out loud something like "I'm totally gorgeous" or "I've got a terrific body" or "I'm really hot—anybody would be lucky to be my lover." Play around with some seductive poses. Do a little dance. Mug it up. Have fun. Keep telling yourself how wonderful and desirable you are. You might feel a little silly at first, but nobody else will witness this display, so throw off your inhibitions.

Shape Your Energy Field

Become aware of the energy field around you. You're already familiar with sensing your aura as a result of the exercises you did in the previous chapter and through working with projections. Now you want to infuse your energy field with the "essence of beauty" with which you've connected. Mentally pour that beauty over your aura, as if you were drizzling a golden layer of maple syrup over yourself. Don't try to cover up flaws—you're putting on a patina, not a mask.

Now, envision yourself working the essence of beauty into your aura, as if you were massaging fragrant oil into your skin. Become one with beauty. Mold it with your thoughts—the same way you'd knead flesh with your fingers—until beauty is interwoven into the material of your aura, not just lying on top of it like plastic wrap on a package of hamburger. Continue thinking and telling yourself how fabulous you are. Believe it, and others will, too. But the moment you let doubt or self-criticism sneak in, your glamour will fade. The spell is broken.

You can cast a glamour for any image you wish to present. If you're giving a speech and want to appear intelligent, witty, and interesting, use the same technique to create the illusion you desire. If want to intimidate an opponent on the gridiron, cast a glamour to make yourself seem bigger, faster, or tougher. Just massage intelligence, toughness, or whatever into your aura instead of beauty.

Like projections, glamours have a short shelf life, usually a few hours to perhaps a day at best. To get the most mileage out of your glamour, put it on the way you would perfume, as close as possible to the time you'll need it—right before that job interview or big date. One of the cool things about a glamour or a projection is that other people can help feed it for you, and it can build on itself. When you start getting positive attention from others, your confidence grows and your emotions elevate, which strengthens your glamour. Those good feelings boost your energy, charge your aura, and keep you in a place of attraction.

You can also use crystals to augment and extend the life of your glamour, just as you did when working with projections. Charge your crystal with your intention, then keep it on your person when you go "on stage."

Creating Lures

Lures fall into territory some people may find objectionable. They're like those subliminal images advertisers hide in TV commercials to influence you subconsciously to buy or do something, without you realizing you've even seen the sneaky image. On *Rob's Magick Blog,* Robert A. Peregrine explains it this way: "A glamour is like wearing nice clothes to make yourself appear more attractive to a girl. A projection is like putting a love song on the radio to put her into a favorable mood. A lure is like slipping pills into her drink so you can rape her."

Before we continue, I'd like to reiterate that I'm not going to tell you whether or not you should attempt to use lures or any other type of magic—that's up to you. My objective is simply to provide information—how, what, when, where, and why—not to moralize. Furthermore, according to the principle of attraction, you only hook up with people and circumstances that are on the same wavelength as you. You can't seduce someone whose resonance doesn't match yours, and you can't take money from someone who isn't energetically predisposed to give it to you—even through the use of manipulative magic.

Magical lures can be quite complex, just as some fishing lures are amazingly intricate. You can devise a quick-acting lure that snags your target immediately, or one whose outcome will slowly evolve over time. When your lure strikes home, it lodges in your target's consciousness and coerces him/her to see things your way. The best part (for you) is that person thinks the ideas you've planted with your lure are actually his/her own.

Planting a Lure

First, turn your attention to your own energy field. Raise your energy through whatever means you prefer. When you've elevated your resonance to the highest level you can achieve at this time, mentally grab a chunk of that energy, just as you might scoop up a handful of snow. Then bury your intention—as a word or image—in the glob of energy and pack energy around your intention, as if you were embedding a stone in a snowball. Simple, direct commands usually work best: hire me; love me; take me on a vacation to St. John; buy me a Mercedes.

You can also plant a lure that doesn't have a specific, clearly defined outcome. This type of lure causes your target to view you in a favorable way. For example, embed an idea such as "[your name]'s intelligence is really impressive" or "[your name] is incredibly attractive" or "everybody thinks [your name] is terrific." Suggestions such as these have the potential to evolve in a number of ways beyond your initial goal.

Add Sex Energy to Your Lure

Now let's add the excitement and immediacy of sex energy to the spell. Using your imagination or employing actual physical stimulus, connect with the feeling of sexual arousal to the point of near orgasm. Spend a few minutes enjoying this sensation, letting it lift you to a high level of excitation. Feel the impetus, the urgency to climax—but don't actually come. Add this intense sexual excitation to the lure.

Then envision yourself hurling the ball of energy that contains your objective at your target. When your energy hits the person you've targeted, s/he will receive your intention along with the sense of urgency and feel compelled to act immediately on that intention.

Magic Knots

Sailors have developed knot-tying into an art form, but not all knots are used for fishing or attaching boats to docks. Long ago, seafarers captured the wind in magic knots. During storms, mariners tied the energy of the wind into rope knots—those bowlines, sheepshanks, and angler's loops had magical as well as practical *raisons d'etre.* If a sailor found himself becalmed at sea he opened a knot, releasing the pent-up wind and filling his sails, so he could continue on his journey.

Tie Your Intentions into Magic Knots

Magic knots provide a simple, yet wonderful way to store energy for future use. The knot holds the energy of the present until sometime down the line when you need it. You can tie any intention into a magic knot. If you want to attract prosperity, for instance, first raise your energy to a positive level by imagining how happy you'd be having an endless supply of wealth coming into your life. Envision enjoying all the beautiful things you'd own, traveling to exotic places for lavish vacations, and so on. You could even go on a window-shopping spree and have fun looking at all the luxuries you plan to own.

Then tie knots into a piece of golden ribbon or cord (gold symbolizes wealth) while you continue to hold these pleasant thoughts in your mind and feel the joyful emotions. The next time you need some cash, open a knot. The energy of abundance will flow out into the universe and attract to you the prosperity you desire.

If you prefer, you can tie knots in a piece of rope and, when you need to access the energy of prosperity, toss the rope into a fire. You might want to build a ritual fire in your cauldron for this purpose. Add to the fire a little cedar wood—it's linked with wealth. As the rope burns, your intentions are released, aided by the activating energy of the fire element. The smoke carries your wishes to the higher realms in the form of prayers to your favorite deities. Tying a knotted string around a candle and allowing the candle to burn down, incinerating the string, will work, too. Just be careful to do this in a safe place so you don't start a house fire in the process.

Store Sex Energy in Magic Knots

My favorite form of knot magic ties sexual energy into the knots. You can do this alone, with a partner, or in a group. First, acquire a piece of rope, cord, or ribbon as long as you are from your toes to your fingertips when you extend your arm up over your head. If you're working with a partner, decide who's going to be the incubating/creative member in a particular spell or ritual (usually the woman) and cut the rope to the length of that person's body. In a group situation, each participant could cut a piece of rope the length of his/her own body and knot it at the appropriate time— unless the group has chosen a primary magician or couple through which to focus the group's energy.

Next, decide on a telos. The rope or cord should be of a color that symbolizes your purpose (see chapter 9). As with all types of sex magic, it's important that everyone involved agrees on the same objective. Then begin the process of arousal. Caress, kiss, lick, suck, employ sex toys—whatever turns you on. Continue building your passion slowly, while keeping your intention in mind. Sustain sexual excitation for as long as you can. Get close to orgasm and then back away numerous times, in order to elevate your energy to the max. (A minimum of three times is recommended, nine times is optimal.) With practice, you'll learn to walk that tightrope and remain on the edge of orgasm for as long as you choose.

When you're finally ready to come, hold the cord and get ready to tie knots. This is one time when you *don't* want to come at the same time your partner does (if you're working with a partner, that is). With male-female couples, it's usually preferable for the woman to reach orgasm first. The man ties knots into the rope—as many as possible—while she comes. The knots capture the energy of her orgasm along with the telos linked to it. Now it's his turn, while she ties knots. Same-sex couples and multiorgasmic people can do whatever suits you best.

Later on, when you want to access the energy tied into the knots, open one of them. If your telos was to attract prosperity, for example, untie a knot when you seek financial gain. You'll feel an instant rush as you release the sexual energy from the knot. You'll also release your intention, which is entwined in the sexual energy, into the universe, where it will resonate through the matrix and draw prosperity to you.

I'm not sure how long you can contain energy in a knot, but my guess is at least as long as you can cellar a good bottle of Cabernet Sauvignon—maybe until the rope itself decays. I have a string of knots I made more than ten years ago, and, having recently opened one of them, I know the energy in them is still potent. During these uncertain times, when you can't rely on the value of real estate, stocks, and other investments, magic knots may offer a way to stash your energetic wealth until you need it in the future.

Permanent Knots

Some knots aren't meant to be opened. They hold your intention *ad infinitum*. Let's say you want to protect your cat, whose curiosity sometimes gets her into trouble. You could tie a protection spell into a knot and attach it to her collar to safeguard her. Are you having doubts about your lover's fidelity? Try sewing magic knots into his clothing to keep him from wandering. Each time you tie a knot, visually place your intention into it.

Magicians often tie knots to bind an enemy. A common spell involves creating an effigy or "poppet" out of wax, straw, cloth, wood, or other material to represent your enemy. If possible, attach bits of the enemy's hair and/or fingernails to the poppet. Or, glue a photo of the person onto the doll. Write his/her name there, too, and say aloud: "Figure of [whatever material you've used], I now name you [your enemy's name]." Then tie the poppet's hands and feet. As you tie each knot, state your intention to bind this person energetically and to hobble your enemy's power. (In my book *Nice Spells/Naughty Spells* you'll find several spells that utilize knot magic.)

nine

Setting
the Stage

Ambiance is the olive in the martini of sex. Candlelight, romantic music, silk sheets strewn with rose petals set the mood and kindle those inner fires. When you're doing sex magic, however, the atmosphere of your magical space should both raise your resonance and focus your attention. By heightening your sensitivity to everything around you and engaging all your senses, you'll expand your ability to receive and give pleasure—and strengthen your magical power.

The accoutrements you choose to bring into your ritual space can offer additional benefits as well. As you set the stage, consider the magical properties and associations of candles, gemstones, scents, sounds, and so on—as well as their aesthetic ones—and utilize them to your advantage.

Candle Magic

A popular tool for many magicians, candles have served practical, spiritual, and magical purposes for thousands of years. More than five millennia ago, the Egyptians fashioned beeswax candles with reed wicks similar to our present-day ones. The term "candle" comes from the Latin word *candere,* which means "to shine."

In mundane as well as magical environments, candles add ambiance—they transform an ordinary space into an enchanted one. We associate soft, flickering candlelight with romance, so naturally candles play a role in setting the stage for sex magic. However, their magical applications are far more extensive. In fact, candles can play a role in virtually any spell or ritual. A burning candle symbolizes the element of fire—which metaphysicians connect with vitality, action, creativity, and passion—as well as spirit. Therefore, lighting candles enlivens your spell and links you to the higher realms. Sirona Knight writes in *Love, Sex, and Magick,* "The flame of the candle represents spirit's highest potential, while the smoke carries your wishes, hopes, and prayers to the divine."

Some Magical Ways to Use Candles

Lighting a novena candle to petition a deity for a blessing is one of the simplest candle spells. You may want to dedicate a candle to a particular god or goddess as a sign of gratitude for providing assistance. Making a wish when you blow out candles on a birthday cake is another easy spell we've all done. Gazing into a candle's flickering flame can help you to focus your attention during a spell, or even induce a light trance. You can also use this technique for scrying, intuitively seeing images in the flame or in the smoke rising from it.

Many magicians place candles on their altars to represent and invoke the fire element or the element of spirit. Additionally, they may choose altar candles to symbolize masculine/god and feminine/goddess energies. Red, orange, gold, or white candles typically stand for masculine energy; blue, green, silver, or black depict the feminine force. In feng shui, candles serve as tools to boost *chi* and enliven some area of your life.

You can tap the activating nature of the fire element by carving an intention into a candle, then lighting it. Use a pointed instrument such as a nail, nail file, or ballpoint pen to engrave a word that expresses what you want to attract: love, money, or success, for instance. If you prefer, etch a symbol into the wax, such as a heart or dollar sign. Then light the candle and let it burn down. The smoke carries your intention into the higher realms as a thought-form that the universe can act upon and bring into the manifest world.

When the melted wax cools, chip it into small pieces and add them to talismans and amulets. (We'll talk more about making and charging talismans and amulets in chapter 11.) If you've done a spell for protection, sprinkle the chips of candle wax around your home to establish a barrier.

Circle Casting with Candles

During a spell or ritual, you may wish to mark the four directions with candles. Place a yellow candle in the east, a red one in the south, a blue one in the west, and a green one in the north. Or, cast a circle by positioning candles completely around the space where you'll perform your spell. Use white or black candles to form the circle, and place yellow, red, blue, and green ones at the four compass points. Start lighting the candles at the east, the yellow one first. Continue lighting the others one by one, moving in a clockwise direction around the circle.

When I do sex magic, I like to arrange twelve candles in a circle around the bed or sacred space where I'm working. The candles form a protective circle and provide seductive illumination. The twelve candles stand for the twelve signs of the zodiac—it's like having a circle of stars around me. Usually, I engrave the candles with symbols of my intent. The sexual energy raised during the ritual will interact with those symbols and empower them, to bring my intentions to fruition. At the end of the spell, I extinguish the candles in the reverse (counterclockwise) direction.

Different Types of Candles

Candles come in a wide range of shapes and sizes, which can be used for various purposes. It's great if you can make your own candles, imprinting them with your magical intentions at each step of the process. However, most of us simply don't have the time to handcraft our candles. For your spells and rituals, try to find candles fabricated from natural materials, such as beeswax or soy with cotton wicks instead of petroleum-based wax with wicks that contain lead.

Before you use a candle in a spell or ritual, wash it with tepid water and mild soap to remove dust as well as ambient energies that might interfere with your purposes. Anoint your candles with essential oils that support your intention (you'll find suggestions later in this chapter). If you wish to attract or increase something, start at the base of the candle and rub the oil toward the tip (but not on the wick); if your goal involves diminishing or banishing, apply oil from the top of the candle downward.

Ordinary tapers—the kind you place on your dining room table—often grace altars and mantels during ceremonies. Pillars burn for a long time, so they're a good choice if you're doing a lengthy ritual or a spell that continues over a period of days. You can carve words and symbols into pillars more easily, too. Votives in glass containers dispense with the need for candleholders; you can burn them more safely outdoors, too, because they're protected from the wind. Lanterns also work well in outdoor settings. Candles in metal tins are great for travelers. You'll even find candles that float in a bathtub, candles in the forms of deities, and candles shaped like penises. These are great for sex magic rituals.

Using Candles in Sympathetic Magic

In sympathetic magic, candles can be used to represent people—a lover or business partner you wish to attract, someone to whom you're sending healing energy, or an enemy you intend to bind. You may designate an ordinary candle to signify a particular person by writing that person's name on the candle, gluing on hair and/or nail clippings taken from the person, or affixing a photo of him/her to the candle. If you prefer, you can purchase a ready-made "poppet" candle shaped like a miniature human or fashion one yourself from wax.

Candle Positions

Some spells involve positioning and moving candles in specified patterns. Others require you to enact a number of steps over a period of time. Spells for beginnings, growth, or attraction might involve placing your candle(s) in the east where the sun rises; spells for endings, decrease, or banishing may call for putting your candle(s) in the west.

Let's say your goal is to attract a lover. Position two red or pink candles about a foot apart on your altar. One candle represents you, the other your prospective partner. Each day, light the candles and move them a little closer together, until they're touching. As you do this spell, imagine you are drawing a lover to you. If you want to push an enemy or rival out of your territory, designate a candle to represent you, then encircle it with eight white candles. Each day, move the circle of candles out a bit more, widening your area of influence, control, and protection.

Most spells recommend allowing the candles to burn down completely or snuffing them rather than blowing them out. I've included many candle spells in my books *Nice Spells/Naughty Spells, The Everything Spells & Charms Book, The Everything Wicca & Witchcraft Book,* and *Good Spells for Bad Days.* You'll also find books devoted entirely to the art of candle magic.

When you cast spells, choose a candle whose color corresponds to your objective. If you're doing a spell to attract a lover, burn red or pink candles that represent passion, love, and affection. "Money colors"—gold, silver, and green—work best for prosperity spells. Different cultures ascribe different meanings to colors, and each of us has certain color preferences and associations. For instance, in the West the general public connects black with death and mourning. However, witches consider black a color of power because it contains all the hues of the visible spectrum.

Choosing the Right Colors for Your Spells

Although the color relationships are mainly symbolic, studies show that color influences us physically, emotionally, and psychologically. Red stimulates us; blue calms us. Yellow has an uplifting effect, whereas brown makes us feel grounded and secure.

Choosing appropriately colored candles for your spells is only part of setting the stage. Consider incorporating meaningful colors into your sacred space with furnishings, linens, rugs, artwork, flowers, and so on. Magicians often wear clothing in colors that represent their intentions or symbolize the theme of a ritual. The colors influence you subconsciously and remind you of your objective.

- *Red:* to increase passion, vitality, courage, or to stimulate action

- *Orange:* for strength, self-confidence, or to heighten your resonance

- *Yellow:* for happiness, creativity, optimism, or to aid communication

- *Green:* for healing, growth, or to attract prosperity

- *Light blue:* to promote peace, improve clarity, or ease pain

- *Royal blue:* to gain insight or spur imagination

- *Indigo:* to stimulate intuition or mental power

- *Purple:* to gain wisdom, connect with higher realms, or strengthen personal power

- *Pink:* to attract or enhance love and friendship

- *White:* for protection or purification

- *Black:* for banishing, binding, or to increase power

- *Brown:* for stability and grounding in the physical world

Working with Crystals and Gemstones

Since ancient times, people throughout the world have tapped the magical powers of crystals and gemstones for a panoply of purposes ranging from protection to attracting love. Early sailors carried sapphires to ensure safe sea voyages. The Romans considered emeralds stones of fertility. The Old Testament describes amethysts as having spiritual power. Plato proposed that "gems owe their origins to the stars." In *The Power of Jewelry,* Nancy Schiffer writes that our ancestors believed gemstones were "capable of human feelings and passions so that they could express jealousy and shock."

Today magicians and healers still prize crystals and other stones for their myriad properties and powers. The stones' resonances interact with your own energy and influence you physically, emotionally, and spiritually. That's why people originally wore birthstones—to balance, enhance, or mitigate certain natal characteristics.

Stones and Their Magical Uses

Each gem is unique, possessing special qualities that can be utilized in spells and rituals of all kinds, as well as for therapeutic purposes. Crystals and gemstones are highly sensitive to the resonances around them, which makes them wonderful agents for magicians casting spells. By combining your powers with those of a particular stone, you can amplify your own magical abilities. The following list suggests gemstones to use for various objectives.

- *Amber:* protection
- *Amethyst:* meditation, dream work, psychic ability
- *Aquamarine:* mental clarity, spiritual insight
- *Aventurine:* prosperity
- *Bloodstone:* strength, physical protection
- *Carnelian:* passion and sexual energy
- *Citrine:* cleansing your energy field, clearing stones and crystals
- *Diamond:* commitment and trust in love relationships
- *Emerald:* healing, growth, mental and emotional balance

- *Hematite:* grounding and stability

- *Jade:* prosperity, good fortune, and health

- *Lapis lazuli:* psychic ability, insight

- *Moonstone:* balancing emotions, dream work

- *Onyx:* banishing negative forces, grounding and stability

- *Opal:* love and affection

- *Pearl:* balance in love relationships

- *Quartz (clear):* holding information, transmitting thoughts/emotions, augmenting the qualities of other stones

- *Red jasper:* passion, healing sexual problems

- *Rose quartz:* love and friendship, healing emotional issues

- *Ruby:* stimulating emotions, courage, strength

- *Sapphire:* spiritual knowledge, wisdom, and insight

- *Smoky quartz:* to hold something until you are ready to deal with it

- *Tiger's eye:* prosperity and success

- *Turquoise:* protection, health, and prosperity

(Excerpted from *The Everything Spells & Charms Book* by Skye Alexander, published by Adams Media 2008)

Gemstones and the Chakras

When choosing stones for spells, consider their colors and opacity. It's usually best to use clear stones when you're dealing with mental and spiritual issues, translucent or cloudy stones for emotional situations, and opaque stones for physical matters. Healers who work with crystals and gemstones associate certain stones with the seven major chakras, or energy centers, in the body. You can position stones directly on your body where your chakras are located in order to balance, strengthen, or unblock vital energy. Select stones whose colors match those of the chakras.

- *Root chakra:* red stones (ruby, garnet, red jasper, red agate)

- *Sacral chakra:* orange stones (carnelian, tangerine quartz, amber)

- *Solar plexus chakra:* yellow stones (topaz, yellow calcite, citrine, yellow amber)

- *Heart chakra:* green stones (emerald, jade, malachite, aventurine, moss agate)

- *Throat chakra:* light blue stones (aquamarine, blue lace agate, blue topaz, turquoise)

- *Brow chakra:* indigo stones (sapphire, lapis lazuli, sodalite)

- *Crown chakra:* purple stones (amethyst, fluorite, sugilite)

Quartz Crystals and Their Properties

Quartz crystals are the most versatile and popular of all stones. Because they retain information, amplify energy, and transmit resonances, crystals are used in watches, TV and radio equipment, and computers. These same properties enable magicians to work with crystals for storing ideas and intentions, sending and attracting energy, protection, healing, divination, and a wealth of other purposes.

When you combine crystals with other stones, they augment the characteristics of those stones. As a general rule, large crystals are more powerful than small ones, but the quality of the crystal and how "awake" it is will also affect its abilities.

Crystals come in many shapes and configurations. The shape influences the way energy moves through the crystal and suggests its best applications.

- Single-terminated crystals have one point, and can attract or send energy in the direction of the point.

- Double-terminated crystals have a point at either end, and can attract or send energy in both directions.

- Abundance crystals contain greenish specks of chlorite, and are often used to attract prosperity.

- Creator crystals have smaller crystals or materials growing inside them; they can help you nurture and birth your intentions.

- Clusters of crystals feature numerous points, all connected at the base; you can program them to work on many different issues, to attract or send energy in various directions, or to handle group issues.

- Crystal balls are often used for scrying and divination.

Many people wear or carry crystals for protection. Put one in your car's glove compartment to keep you safe while driving. Add one to your carry-on bag when you fly. Plant crystals in your yard to safeguard your property. You can place crystals in a circle around the space where you perform a magic spell or ritual. This serves two purposes: it keeps the energy you raise during your spell inside the circle and prevents unwanted energies from interfering.

Before you work with a crystal, clear it of ambient resonances or any intentions that may have been put into it by someone else. Crystals pick up the vibrations in their environment, too. When I visited the office of a friend who's a psychotherapist, I noticed the crystals on his altar were dull and cloudy. They'd witnessed so many painful and stormy emotional sessions among his patients that they'd shut down. My friend didn't realize he needed to clear them regularly to remove all that unpleasant energy. Use the instructions in chapter 8 to clear your crystals before working magic with them.

Using Crystals in Sex Magic

In the last chapter, we talked about using crystals to extend the life of a projection or glamour. But crystals offer you much more—their magical uses may be limited only by your imagination. Because crystals are so sensitive to resonance, and because they hold onto the vibes you place in them for a very long time, they're ideal adjuncts to sex magic. My personal opinion is they love the joyful and passionate energy raised during sex and revel in it—after all, crystals can't do it themselves, so the only way they can partake of the pleasure is through osmosis.

· When you're doing sex magic, circle the bed, room, or other area with crystals—they'll provide protection. The crystal circle will also amplify the energy you raise and radiate it back to you, boosting your magical power.

· Keep crystals near you while engaging in sex magic, so you can impart your energy and intentions to the stones. They'll readily absorb the high resonance of excitation, along with your thoughts and emotions, and retain these energies for a long time. (Do you see the crystals sparkling more brightly now?)

· To promote healing, lay a crystal on a particular part of your body or chakra where you want to direct healing energy. At the moment of orgasm, mentally focus your energy and intention into the impaired area—the crystal will assist you.

· After you've raised your energy and reached a high level of excitation, gently stroke your body with a crystal. Allow the crystal to absorb the powerful resonance you're emitting. I don't recommend inserting a crystal into any orifice, however—these guys are sharp, remember. (If you're into that, consider using a smooth, shiva lingam stone instead.)

· After imbuing your crystals with passion and intention, wear or carry them to bring you whatever you desire. Or, place them where they'll best serve your purpose: in your purse to attract money, on your nightstand to attract a lover, by your front door to repel intruders, and so on.

· Add sexually charged crystals to talisman or amulet bags. In chapter 11 we'll go into detail about making talismans, amulets, and other charms.

· Set a charged crystal on your altar to enhance the power of any spell or ritual. The crystal will continue doing whatever you've programmed it to do, even after you've finished the spell or ritual.

· Give charged crystals to other people to assist them in obtaining their desires.

These are only a few suggestions. As you continue working with crystals and sex magic, you'll undoubtedly think of other ways to utilize these energies to manifest the outcomes you seek. Keep your crystals in a safe place when you're not using them and don't let anyone else handle your crystals—the crystals will pick up that person's energies.

Scent-sational Sex

Four millennia ago on the island of Cyprus—home to Aphrodite, goddess of love and beauty—the Greeks were making perfume. But the Egyptians had already bested them by two thousand years, formulating aromatic concoctions for everything from seduction to embalming. Legend has it that Cleopatra announced her meeting with Mark Anthony by scenting the sails of her ship. Today, fragrance is a multi-billion-dollar-a-year industry.

The brain reacts to scent in .05 seconds, faster than it does to pain. Smelling a scent affects the limbic system of your brain—the part that controls emotion and sexuality—triggering feelings and/or physical responses. According to

Rachel Herz, author of *The Scent of Desire*, "above all other physical characteristics, women ranked a man's scent as the most important feature for determining whether she would be sexually interested in him."

Seductive Essences

The vast majority of fragrances on the market today are synthetic chemical brews, but you'll get more bang for your buck with essential oils. Essential oils give plants their distinctive scents. Peel an orange and its aroma spritzes forth. Rub a rosemary sprig between your hands and the plant's fragrance perfumes your palms. Essential oils can be obtained from the flowers, leaves, bark, roots, seeds, and resins of the plant. Sometimes considered the "life blood" of the plant, essential oils contain natural vital energy that can empower your spells as well as ignite your passion. Only pure essential oils possess this energy, though. Synthetic substances (regardless of their tantalizing names) are as lifeless as an inflatable sex doll.

Just as everyone has distinct food preferences, different people prefer different scents. However, some aromas have long been associated with kindling passion, romance, and eroticism. These include:

- Amber
- Bergamot
- Clove
- Cinnamon
- Gardenia
- Jasmine

- Musk

- Orange blossom

- Patchouli

- Rose

- Vanilla

- Ylang-ylang

How can you summon up the seductive powers of essential oils? Many oils can be used just like perfume—simply dab a little on your throat, wrists, or other pulse points on your body. Rub a little between your breasts, on the insides of your thighs, or your lower belly. Because some oils can cause skin irritations or allergic reactions, test them in small amounts to see how you react and don't use them full strength.

Blend one or more of these essential oils into your favorite massage oil or lotion, or mix them with pure olive, grape seed, or jojoba oil. Then treat your partner and yourself to a sensual massage to rev up your desire. If you prefer, soak in a hot bath to which you've added erotic essential oils such as patchouli, ylang-ylang, or jasmine. Sex magic rituals often begin with a special bath to help you wash away everyday cares and shift your awareness from the mundane to the magical realm. According to Hippocrates, often regarded as the father of Western medicine, "The path to health is a scented bath and a daily massage."

Dressing Candles with Essential Oils

Candles, too, can be treated or "dressed" with essential oils. This practice of anointing with scented oils not only triggers your libido, it also brings the plant's natural energy into your spell.

Pour a little oil into your palm and rub it onto the candle's surface, covering everything except the wick. As mentioned earlier, rub oil from the base of the candle toward the tip if you wish to attract or expand something, or rub from the top down if your goal is to reduce, release, or bind. If you plan to engrave a symbol or word into the wax, do it before you dress the candle with oil.

You can purchase candles already scented with essential oils—note, however, that most scented candles do not contain pure essential oils and therefore lack the magical energies of plants. They won't stimulate your senses in the same way either.

Seductive Sounds

Do the songs of old "torch" singers and crooners such as Billie Holiday, Mel Tormé, and Frank Sinatra put you in the mood for love? Maybe you prefer the romantic ballads of Garth Brooks or the soulful blues of Janis Joplin. Or perhaps you get hot listening to the spicy sounds of salsa, tango, and flamenco music.

Music and sex have been paired since ancient times. The *Kama Sutra* emphasizes the importance of playing musical instruments, singing, and dancing in the art of lovemaking. Today you need only watch some music videos to see how the contemporary music industry links sex and music.

Rev Up Your Resonance with Music

However, seductive songs aren't the only type of music to play when you're setting the stage for sex magic. Remember, the better you feel the more powerful your magical and magnetic ability. If you're like many people, listening to music lifts your spirits and raises your resonance. According to Jonathan Goldman, director of the Sound Healers Association, "sound create[s] balance and alignment in the physical body, the energy centers called 'chakras,' and/or the etheric fields. Sound healing is a vibrational therapy and can be understood as being energy medicine." Other researchers have found that the music of Mozart influences the body in a positive way and can produce beneficial effects, whereas the impact of rap and heavy metal tends to be detrimental.

Goldman and other sound healers associate the seven notes on the musical scale with the body's seven major chakras. Playing or intoning a note whose resonance matches that of a particular chakra can help to balance, unblock, and strengthen that chakra. The sacral chakra, which affects the sex organs, corresponds to the musical note D. Singing bowls made of crystal or metal are tuned to different notes. To enhance the functioning of the sacral chakra, you could play a singing bowl tuned to D—you can even lie down and set the bowl on your abdomen, enabling the bowl's resonance to interact directly with your body. This technique not only provides healing in the sex organs, it stimulates sexual energy and helps raise your personal resonance.

Drum Up Life Energy

Drumming, too, can elevate your resonance and stimulate the flow of life energy through your system. Many rituals include drumming to raise and harmonize the energies of the participants. The rhythmic, reverberating beat establishes a pattern that guides the mood and direction of a ritual. Playing a drum can also break up "stuck" energy and clear unwanted vibrations from sacred space.

Since antiquity, drumming has served as a form of communication. In West African tradition, each rhythm has its own unique meaning. You can play a specific rhythm to enhance your power, to overcome fears, or to announce a beautiful woman's entrance into the room. Celtic warriors used drums to raise and unite the energies of soldiers entering into battle.

Drumming puts you into a light trance, which is a better place from which to do magic than your ordinary waking level of consciousness. It connects you with the deities and spirits who abide in the nonphysical realms, and lets you summon these entities to assist you in your magical workings. When you play a drum, close your eyes and listen carefully—you'll hear these spirits singing along with you.

You can "drum up" energy and send it wherever you want it to go—even over long distances. Drumming can also activate talismans and amulets. Simply fasten the charm to the drum or paint on the drum a symbol that represents your intention. As you play, envision the drumbeats carrying your wishes into the matrix, where the universe can act on them.

Flower Power

Flowers not only bring beauty into your magical space, they lend their own vital energy to your spell or ritual. For centuries, herbalists, homeopaths, aromatherapists, and other holistic healers have tapped the life energy in plants to promote well-being in humans. Druids believe trees possess special qualities and powers. Magicians, especially green witches, often work with the resonances of plants to produce outcomes. Each plant has its own properties and magical associations, so you may wish to decorate your ritual space with botanicals that relate to your objectives.

Flowers and Their Magical Associations

This list shows some familiar flowers and their magical correspondences. Consider including them in your spells and rituals to support your intentions.

- *Love:* rose (red or pink), primrose, red clover, myrtle, violet, gardenia, jasmine, orchid, ylang-ylang, apple blossom, peach blossom

- *Prosperity:* lilac, money plant, mint, sunflower, marigold, columbine, daffodil

- *Protection:* snapdragon (white), basil, peony (white), foxglove (caution: poisonous), wolfsbane (caution: poisonous)

- *Career success:* dahlia, sunflower, marigold, daffodil, carnation, buttercup

- *Public image/self-esteem:* narcissus, jonquil, daisy

- *Communication/mental ability:* honeysuckle, azalea, iris

· *Intuition/psychic powers:* lilac, wisteria, lotus, yarrow, violet, lavender, lily of the valley, geranium

· *Banishing:* rosemary, sage, wolfsbane (caution: poisonous)

Tapping the Magic of Plants

You can tap the magical power of flowers and other botanicals by keeping potted plants in your sacred space. Set a vase of fresh flowers on your altar or elsewhere in the area where you do magic. Make sure the plants you choose to display relate to your intentions. Fresh flowers, particularly red roses, add a romantic and sensual touch that can enhance sex magic. When you think about it, flowers are inherently sexy—they unabashedly display their sex organs for all to see.

Dried flowers may be added to talismans and amulets, or blended into candle wax. Edible flowers can enhance ritual soups, salads, or brews. If you have room, grow your favorite plants in a magical garden.

Put a few drops of flower essences in water and drink it from your magic chalice as part of your ritual. Choose borage or gentian to lift your spirits; alpine lily, basil, and/ or hibiscus to increase sexual responsiveness and expression. If you or your partner have any specific sexual issues or requirements, do some research into the properties of flower remedies before using them to find essences that will best serve your needs. (You can purchase flower essences at many health food stores or online at www.flowersociety.org and at www.bachflower.com.)

Offering Flowers to Deities

If you're working with a specific deity in a spell, choose flowers that appeal to him or her. When you request favors from a particular god or goddess, making an offering of flowers is a nice way to say "thanks." You can place flowers on your altar or burn candles that contain flower petals and/or essential oils.

- *Aphrodite:* apple blossoms, roses
- *Apollo:* sunflowers
- *Eros:* roses
- *Freya:* daisies, primrose
- *Hera:* apple blossoms, irises
- *Isis:* irises, heather, roses
- *Juno:* lilies
- *Kuan Yin:* lilies, water lilies
- *Odin:* apple blossoms
- *Thor:* daisies
- *Venus:* roses
- *Zeus:* violets, apple blossoms

Flower Divination

Did you know roses can serve as an oracle? The practice is known as Phyllorhodomancy. Cut three roses that haven't bloomed yet and put them in a vase of water. Ask your question and assign an "answer"—yes, no, or maybe—to each rose. The rose that lasts the longest signifies your answer. (My book *The Everything Wicca & Witchcraft Book* contains more about plant magic.)

Creating a Magical Zone

When interior decorators and feng shui practitioners design a living or work space they carefully consider every item and feature, blending them in a manner that promotes harmony and serves the needs of the people who will utilize the space. Each ingredient has a purpose, and each must complement the others in order to produce the desired effect. When you set the stage for sex magic, you do the same thing.

As you assess what will become your sacred space, ask yourself a few basic questions. Is it comfortable and inviting? Is it private and secure, a place where you can let down your guard and perform magic without being disturbed or observed? If this is an area you use for mundane activities, are you willing and able to transform it (at least temporarily) into a magical site?

For many people, the bedroom is the logical place to enact sex magic rituals. But your bedroom can't function as a pleasure zone or a sacred space if it's full of everyday distractions. Remove, disable, disguise, or otherwise denature anything that might intrude into your magical space—especially electronic devices. Turn off the TV and computer, and cover them with a decorative cloth or screen. Shut down your laptop and phone(s) and put them in a closet, drawer, or other place out of sight. (In *The 30-Day Sex Solution*, authors Victoria and John Wilson recount a frightening statistic: "37 percent of Americans take their laptops to bed with them, and 30 percent interrupt sex to answer their cell phones." Yikes!)

Next, clear the area of anything that detracts from the magical ambiance you're trying to create. Pick up dirty clothes. Relocate books, paperwork, alarm clocks, and other objects that remind you of your outside life. Put family photos, kids' drawings, pet beds/toys, et cetera someplace else for the time being.

Once you've covered these bases, decide on your magical objective. Each telos may require somewhat different "props." For instance, if your goal is to attract money, the colors green, gold, and/or silver should predominate. If you're doing magic to enhance love, surround yourself with red and pink. It might not be practical to paint the walls or install new carpeting for each spell, but you could purchase sheets in colors that correspond to your intentions.

Next, select candles to illuminate your sacred space. Again, choose colors that signify your telos. If you can find candles scented with essential oils that support your objective, great. Otherwise, purchase aromatic oil(s) separately and dress the candles prior to enacting your sex magic ritual.

In my opinion, these are the fundamentals, but anything you can do to transform your ordinary reality into a mystical realm will enhance the power of your magic. If something particularly turns you on—music, for instance—by all means include it. Add any or all of the following, according to your personal preferences:

- Clothing that gets you and your partner in the mood for sex magic

- Flowers that convey your intention

- Sensuous incense

- Sexy music

- Erotic artwork and magic sigils

- Crystals charged to assist you in amplifying and focusing your energy

- Cool sex toys and great lubes

- Luscious massage oils

- Tantalizing foods and beverages

You don't have to invest a lot of money to create a sexual Shangri-La. However, the enthusiasm, effort, and energy you put into the endeavor will pay off.

Visual Tools
and Techniques

Admittedly, it can be a bit difficult to focus your mind on getting a job or acing an exam when you're riding the waves of sexual ecstasy. That's why sex magicians often rely on visual aids to keep their objectives right before their eyes. It's a whole lot easier to gaze at a meaningful image at the moment of orgasm than to utter a well-phrased affirmation. And, as we've already discussed, pictures can convey your intentions more clearly and profoundly than words.

The Magic of the Tarot

Most people use the tarot (pronounced tah ROE) to divine the future or to gain insight into a particular concern or situation. This most beautiful of oracles typically contains seventy-eight illustrated cards, divided into two sections or "books" known as the major arcana and the minor arcana. *Arcana* means mysteries or secrets.

A strong connection exists between magic and the tarot. For starters, the minor arcana, which bears similarities to our ordinary poker deck, consists of fifty-six numbered cards organized into four suits that depict the four primary tools in a magician's toolbox: wands, pentacles/pentagrams, cups/chalices, and swords/daggers. The twenty-two cards of the major arcana present archetypal and mythical images, along with a wealth of esoteric knowledge that's been handed down through the ages. Card #1 is even called The Magician and portrays a magus with his four magic tools. The major arcana also describes a course of initiation that guides the seeker from innocence to enlightenment. (My book *The Everything Tarot Book* offers more extensive information about the tarot.)

Spellworking with the Tarot

Magicians often use tarot cards in spellworking as well as for divination. Some schools of magic, such as the Golden Dawn, encourage a thorough understanding of the tarot. Two of the most popular tarot decks, the Rider-Waite deck and the Thoth deck, were designed by noted magicians Arthur Edward Waite and Pamela Colman Smith, and Aleister Crowley respectively.

The rich colors, imagery, and other symbolism on tarot cards make them ideal for visualization and conveying intentions. The suit of pentacles, for example, represents money and material goods. Cups signify love, emotions, and relationships. Wands connote creative endeavors and career pursuits. Swords relate to ideas and communication. If your objective is to attract a romantic partner or improve an existing relationship, you could incorporate the two of cups or the Lovers card into a spell. If you'd like to increase your income, you might choose to work with the nine of pentacles. The following list suggests some tarot cards to use for various purposes:

- *To attract money:* ace, three, nine, or ten of pentacles; Wheel of Fortune

- *To attract a lover:* ace or two of cups; The Lovers, The Emperor (male), The Empress (female)

- *To improve a romantic relationship:* two, six, or ten of cups; The Lovers

- *To get a new job or start a new business venture:* ace of wands, ace of pentacles

- *For career success:* six of wands, The Emperor, The Empress, Wheel of Fortune, The Sun, The World

- *To attract fame or recognition:* The Star, The Sun, The World

- *For health:* nine of cups, nine of wands, Strength, Temperance

- *To attract friends and positive social connections:* three of cups

- *For joint business/financial ventures:* six of pentacles

- *To overcome obstacles:* Strength

- *For travel:* knight of wands, six of swords

- *For good luck in any area:* nine of cups, Wheel of Fortune, The Star, The World

- *For intuition or insight:* The High Priestess, The Moon

- *For peace or congeniality:* Temperance

- *For domestic happiness or to get a home:* ten of cups

- *For legal issues:* Justice, Judgement

Using the Tarot in Sex Magic

Now let's combine the tarot with sex magic. First, find a deck of cards that speaks to you. Although the basic meanings and symbolism are pretty consistent from deck to deck, the imagery on some decks will appeal to you more than others. Hundreds of different decks exist, many of them based on specific themes, spiritual traditions, or cultures. Lori Walls' deliciously naughty *Tarot Erotica* depicts all sorts of sexual acts and imagery—you may find it exciting to work with when you do sex magic. Some magicians designate one deck for readings and another for doing magic. If you're working with a new deck, cleanse it beforehand by holding it in the smoke of burning sage or incense for a few moments. Then blow on the deck to imprint it with your energy.

Choose a card that most closely depicts your telos. Spend a few moments looking at the card, absorbing its meaning, and linking your intention to the card. Think about the outcome you desire to produce. Allow the card's symbolism to speak to you. While you're doing this you may receive insights or impressions that relate to your purposes—make note of them to consider later.

When you're ready, take the card with you into the space where you'll perform your magic. Keep it nearby while you engage in the process of sexual arousal. The card symbolizes your intention and continues to remind you of your telos as you become increasingly more excited. At the moment of orgasm, simply stare at the picture on the card to project your intention, fueled by your sexual energy, out into the universe. Now that was easy, wasn't it?

Rune Magic

The runes, too, can serve as visual aids in spells. *Rune* means a secret or mystery. The best known of these ancient symbols come from the old Teutonic alphabet and represent objects, conditions, qualities, or deities. Early people carved runes on bone, wood, or stones, however, today you can also find them etched on gemstones and printed on cards.

Spellworking with the Runes

Like the tarot, the runes are most often used as an oracle, but you can include them in spells as well. Carve them on candles, wear them as jewelry, or add them to talismans and amulets. When I went to Stonehenge, I cast tiny runes made from silver and gold into the center of the great stone circle.

The following list suggests runes you could use in spells to produce various outcomes. (Please note that the rune names given here come from Ralph Blum's *The Book of RuneCards.* Other sources spell them differently.)

- *To attract money:* inguz, jera, fehu, dagaz

- *To attract a lover or improve a romantic relationship:* gebo

- *To get a new job or start a new venture:* berkana

- *For career success or advancement:* inguz, jera, fehu, berkana

- *For protection:* algiz, eihwaz

- *For travel:* raido, ehwaz

- *For happiness and good times:* wunjo

- *For health:* uruz, laguz

- *For strength or courage:* uruz, teiwaz

- *For good luck:* dagaz, wunjo, inguz

Using Runes in Sex Magic

Like tarot cards, runes can be used as visual aids in sex magic. Choose one or more runes that represent your telos and bring the rune(s) into your ritual space. (Remember to cleanse it beforehand.) As you become aroused, look at the rune and let it imprint its meaning on your subconscious. You can even finger-paint runes on your body and your lover's. A lover once tantalized me by covering my body from head to foot with red Xs (the rune for love). Gaze at the rune during orgasm and let your sexual power launch your objective into the matrix. Your subconscious remembers the symbol's meaning, even if your conscious mind has melted down.

Other Magical Alphabets and Symbols

When we speak of the runes, most people think of the familiar and popular Norse runes. However, you can use Celtic *Ogham* runes, Egyptian hieroglyphs, kanji symbols, or glyphs from other languages in the same way. Bill Whitcomb's book *The Magician's Companion* includes charts of Hebrew, Coptic, Sanskrit, Tibetan, and other alphabets that may intrigue you. The important thing is that the symbols speak to you and you feel comfortable working with them. You can even create your own magic language.

The I Ching

The hexagrams of the *I Ching* or Book of Changes are good choices, too. Reputed to have been created by Confucius 3,000 years ago, the *I Ching* (pronounced EE Ching) contains sixty-four patterns called hexagrams, each composed of six lines stacked one on top of the other. Like runes and the tarot, the *I Ching* is most often consulted as an oracle for divination or for guidance in a particular situation. Each hexagram has a particular meaning. (The bestselling English translation is the Wilhelm-Baynes edition, published by Princeton University Press, but you'll find many other versions as well, some of them written in more contemporary, accessible language.)

Spellworking with the I Ching

You can also utilize I Ching symbols in magic spells, just as you would tarot cards or runes. First, read the meanings of the various hexagrams and decide which one most closely fits your telos. For example, you might choose hexagram 11, T'ai or Peace, to help resolve a conflict with a loved one, coworker, or enemy. Hexagram 42, I or Increase, might be appropriate for a prosperity spell.

Magically, hexagrams can be used in the same ways as runes. Draw one on a piece of paper and add it to a talisman or amulet. Or, hang the design in a place where you'll see it often to remind yourself of your objective. Carve it on a candle. Include it in a mandala or vision board. Engrave it on a piece of jewelry or embroider it on a garment. Paint one on a plain glass, add water and let the image imprint the water for several minutes, then drink the water.

Using Hexagrams in Sex Magic

When doing sex magic, use hexagrams as visual tools, like runes and tarot cards. Display the design in one or more places where you can see it easily during sex and gaze at it when you orgasm. Because these simple line images are easy to draw, they're fun to finger-paint on your lover's body and/or your own.

Magic Sigils

Have you ever wanted to write in a secret language? You can. A sigil is a written symbol you create for a magical purpose. Your telos is contained within the sigil. Only you can understand the code. If you're working with a magical partner or group, share the secret with them, so you're in agreement about your goal.

Designing a Sigil

The easiest method for designing a sigil uses letters to form an image. Choose a word that represents your intention, such as love, prosperity, health, or success. If you like, you can even compose a short affirmation. Then write the letters on a piece of paper, stacking, entwining, overlaying, or wrapping them around one another to form an image. If your word or phrase contains any duplicated letters, omit the extra letters—you only need one S in success, for instance. Draw the letters right side up, upside down, forward, backward—anyway that appeals to you. Use block or script letters, uppercase or lowercase, or a combination. Add colors that correspond to your intention.

Love   *Success*

Like rune glyphs, sigils have numerous possible applications in magic. Carve them on candles, wear them as jewelry, or add them to talismans and amulets. Hang your sigil on the wall where you'll see it often. Or, frame it and display it on your altar. Lay it on your altar and set a crystal on top of the design to attract or project whatever the sigil conveys. Embroider it onto magical clothing or an altar cloth. I often incorporate sigils into my paintings. You can even tape a sigil to a glass of water (with the image facing in) to imprint the water with your telos. Then drink the water from you chalice and share it with your partner.

Using Sigils in Sex Magic

Before engaging in sex magic, design your sigil. Creating the sigil is a magical act in itself; undertake the process accordingly. If you'll be working with a partner, do this together. I recommend casting a circle and working within it, focusing your mind completely on your task and projecting your intention into the sigil as you design it. Draw the sigil large enough that you can see it easily.

Photocopy it several times and hang the images around your ritual space—on the walls, ceiling, floor, the headboard of your bed—so that no matter what position you're in you'll be able to see the sigil. You can even draw the sigil on one another's bodies.

Begin the process of arousal. Gaze at the sigil frequently as you intensify your excitement. Because you've posted your sigil in a number of spots, you'll be reminded of your intention and reinforce it every time you see the design. At the moment of orgasm, focus on the sigil and let your energy propel the image and your telos into the universe.

Magic Squares

You can also create a sigil on a magic square. Called *kamea* in Hebrew, a magic square is a grid composed of rows and columns of smaller squares. Each of the small squares contains a number. Whether you add the numbers across, down, or diagonally, the sum is always the same. Magic squares relate to the sun, moon, and planets. When you work with a square, you connect with the energy of its corresponding heavenly body. If your objective involves love or relationships, you could use a Venus square. For career success, a sun or Jupiter square might be your best choice. (My book *Magickal Astrology* shows the squares for the sun, moon, Mercury, Venus, Mars, Jupiter, and Saturn.)

The simplest is the Saturn square, a grid made up of nine smaller squares (see illustration). Each column, row, and diagonal adds up to fifteen. Because Saturn governs the material world, this square can help you bring your dreams down to earth and manifest them in the physical plane.

4	9	2
3	5	7
8	1	6

Designing a Sigil on a Magic Square

Choose a word that describes your intention. Then translate the letters into their numerological equivalents, using the following chart.

1	2	3	4	5	6	7	8	9
A	B	C	D	E	F	G	H	I
J	K	L	M	N	O	P	Q	R
S	T	U	V	W	X	Y	Z	

Let's say you want to attract money. The letters in MONEY correspond to the numbers 4, 6, 5, 5, 7. Lay a sheet of tracing paper on top of the magic square, and on the paper draw a small circle anywhere in the square that contains the number 4. (Don't draw the square itself.) Next, draw a line to the square numbered 6. Continue in this manner with the rest of the numbers/letters in your word. Don't double back on the same path, as you are trying to create a distinctive shape. At the end of the final line, draw another small circle.

Sometimes two letters that are positioned next to each other in your word have the same number equivalent, and therefore would fall in the same square, as is the case with N and E (both 5s). If this happens, mark > < on the line where it crosses the square containing that number, which here occurs in square number 5.

Now, add together all the numbers that correspond to the letters in your word: $4 + 6 + 5 + 5 + 7 = 27$. Add the digits in the sum to "reduce" the number to one found on the grid: $2 + 7 = 9$. Draw a small square on the tracing paper in square 9. The finished drawing forms a sigil that represents your intention—a design only you can interpret.

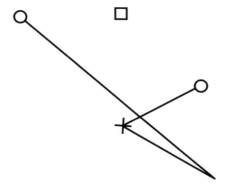

Using Crystals with Magic Squares

Another technique for working with magic squares incorporates the energy of crystals to attract what you desire. Although you could select any magic square, for simplicity let's continue with the Saturn square. Collect nine crystals, one for each of the smaller squares in the grid. Clear the crystals before using them, according to the instructions in the previous chapter.

Next, compile a list of nine things you wish to manifest. Assign a number to each intention. While holding an image of your first intention in your mind, pick up a crystal and blow your telos into it. Set the crystal on the square numbered 1. Blow the second intention on your list into a second crystal, and then place it on square number 2. Continue in this manner until you've programmed and positioned all nine crystals.

Cover the crystals and the magic square with a piece of cloth overnight. In the morning, remove the cover and thank the crystals for their assistance. Your nine intentions are now released into the matrix.

Add Sex Energy to the Magical Mix

Engage in sex near the spot where you've set up the crystals on the square. At the moment of orgasm, gaze at the crystals and project your energy to them. (You may see them sparkle with delight!) Then cover the crystals and the magic square with a piece of cloth and leave them overnight, allowing your spell to gestate. In the morning, remove the cover and thank the crystals for their assistance. Your nine intentions are now released into the matrix.

Magic Numbers

In the world of magic, numbers aren't merely for keeping score. Each number resonates with a unique energy that you can harness in a spell or ritual. Remember the numbers on tarot cards? They're not random or coincidental—they're an essential part of the cards' meanings. Once you understand the secret nature of numbers you can use them as you would any other symbol.

Numbers and Their Secret Meanings

The following list shows the meanings generally associated with the different numbers. Choose the number that represents your intention and tap its energy in spellworking.

    1: beginnings, individuality

    2: partnership, polarity, balance

    3: self-expression, growth

    4: stability, structure

    5: movement, change

    6: cooperation, harmony, beauty

7: rest, withdrawal, the inner world

8: the material world, manifestation

9: abundance, completion, the spiritual realm

Spellworking with Numbers

Let's say your telos involves a relationship. The number of partnerships is two, so it symbolizes your intention. Here are some ideas for incorporating numbers into spells. For simplicity, we'll just consider love spells and the number two here, but you could use these suggestions for other types of spells by substituting the appropriate numbers.

- Burn two candles to express your intention.

- Make a talisman using a silk pouch and slip two objects into it that symbolize love (two small hearts, for example).

- Write the number 2 on a piece of paper and display it in a prominent spot in your home or workplace.

- Include the number 2 in a sigil you design for love.

- Slip two rings on a ribbon and tie it to your bedroom doorknob, using two knots into which you've placed your intention.

- Lay the two of cups from a tarot deck on your altar and set a quartz crystal on top of the card.

- If you know feng shui, place two objects that represent love, such as two roses, in your home's relationship guardian.

Combine numbers with other symbols or objects to fine-tune your spell. For example, if the relationship is a romantic one, burn pink or red candles, or put two pieces of quartz—one rose and one tangerine—into a red or pink talisman pouch. If you're doing a spell for a financial relationship or business partnership, use green candles or abundance crystals instead.

Incorporate Numbers into Sex Magic

After you've determined which number best relates to your intention, include that number in your ritual space, in whatever ways you prefer. I suggest at least using candles of the appropriate number. If you're also doing knot magic, you might consider tying the number of knots that corresponds to your telos. Or, have that number of orgasms. Use your imagination.

Mandalas

Mandala means "circle" in Sanskrit. Most mandalas—but not all—are circular designs containing archetypal, spiritual, metaphorical, and/or personal images that their creators find meaningful. Traditional Hindu and Buddhist mandalas often feature deities or bodhisattvas. Some mandalas symbolically depict the universe—the upper half represents the sky and the lower half the earth—and express humanity's relationship to the cosmos. Others are divided into four quarters to signify the four compass directions or the four elements (earth, air, fire, and water).

Usually mandalas are painted, but you can fabricate one from whatever material you prefer. Zen monks "paint" intricate mandalas using colored sand; the temporary nature of these mandalas emphasizes the importance of the process, not just the goal.

Creating a Magical Mandala

With a little patience, you can make a mandala for magical purposes. Your magic mandala is similar to a vision board that contains images of things you wish to attract into your life. It may address many ideas and goals, or only one. Draw, paint, or paste pictures from magazines within your circle. If you wish, divide it into halves, quarters, or even twelve sections like a horoscope wheel. Feng shui's *bagua* with its nine sectors, each corresponding to a different facet of your life, also provides a good format for a mandala.

Choose colors that represent your intentions. Pink and red should dominate in a mandala for attracting love and passion. Emphasize green, gold, and silver in a prosperity mandala. Add meaningful words, numbers, totem animals, astrological motifs, sigils—whatever appeals to you.

The ritual of creating the mandala is just as important as the finished product—the act is a spell itself. If you're working with a partner or group, consider making this a joint endeavor. As you design and fabricate your mandala, keep your mind focused on the work. Project your objectives into the mandala and imbue it with your energy. Give your imagination free rein. Engage your emotions in the process. Have fun.

Using a Mandala in Sex Magic

When you've finished, display your mandala in a place where you will see it often and let it remind you of your intentions. Hang it above your altar if you like. The mandala incorporates your telos in its imagery. When you do sex magic, position the mandala prominently in your ritual space, perhaps above your bed or wherever you engage in sex. You might want to photocopy it and hang the design in various places around the area, so you can see it no matter what position you're in.

Begin the process of arousal as you gaze at the mandala. Your subconscious will pick up and comprehend the symbols—and your intention(s). At the moment of orgasm, focus your attention on the mandala and allow your energy to propel the intention(s) depicted on it into the universe.

eleven

Amulets, Talismans, and Other Charms

Long before recorded time, people around the world relied on charms of all kinds to ward off evil, to solicit assistance from the gods, to attract good fortune, and for a host of other reasons. Amulets and talismans, totems and tokens, medicine bags and fetishes offered hope to our ancestors as they grappled with the mysterious forces operating in their lives.

The early Egyptians, for instance, tucked magic amulets into the bandages of mummies to aid the deceased in the afterlife. The Chinese affixed "five poison" charms (coin-sized amulets with etchings usually depicting snakes, scorpions, toads, centipedes, and spiders or lizards) to their gates and dwellings to protect themselves and their families.

Ancient Greek and Roman soldiers going into battle carried amulets set with bloodstones, which they believed would prevent serious injury and staunch the flow of blood from wounds. "Evil eye" charms have kept watch over the Turks for millennia. Even rock carvings and cave paintings, such as the 17,000-year-old animal depictions in the caves of Lascaux, France, might have been created for magical purposes, perhaps to petition the gods for success in hunting.

Sacred and secular charms still abound in our modern world. We're all familiar with the auspicious properties of shamrocks, rabbits' feet, and lucky pennies. The Christian cross, the Seal of Solomon, and the Muslim Ta'wiz serve as fetishes for religious seekers who wish to attract divine blessings. Even those sweaty socks athletes wear for weeks without washing in the hope of prolonging a winning streak possess talismanic dimensions.

Basically, a charm is anything to which you ascribe special powers. It may be something you find coincidentally, something you make yourself, something you purchase ready-made, or something given to you by another person. It may be as simple as a shell you pick up on the beach or as rare as a treasured heirloom that's been in your family for seven generations.

Verbal Charms

Although today we use the word "charm" loosely to refer to all sorts of magic spells, early charms were verbal—the easiest type of spell to cast. Far back in the mists of time, shamans or priest/esses may have uttered arcane phrases to call upon deities for assistance or to cast out demons. Then, as now, words possessed power. The word everyone associates with magic—abracadabra—comes from *Avarah K'Davarah,* an Aramaic term that means "I will create as I speak."

Types of Spoken Charms

Spoken charms remain among the most popular of all magic spells. You can proclaim a verbal spell by itself, or combine one with any other spell or ritual. Frequently used verbal spells include:

- *Affirmations:* short, positive statements, worded in the present tense

- *Incantations:* rhymed affirmations

- *Prayers:* requests to a deity for assistance, either for yourself or someone else

- *Blessings:* good wishes, usually offered to someone else

- *Chants:* repeated words or phrases designed to shift mental awareness

- *Invocations:* invitations to a deity to enter your body for a particular purpose

- *Evocations:* commands to spirits requesting their presence and aid

- *Banishments:* orders to spirits and/or other entities to depart and/or desist

- *Bindings:* directives that curtail another's power

- *Curses:* declarations of ill will toward others

Why Verbalize in Rituals and Spells?

Many rituals incorporate one or more of the above charms. Why bother speaking aloud in a spell or ritual if all you really need to do is think or visualize your intention?

Verbal directives can help you stay focused and on track while casting a spell, especially if more than one person is involved. In a group ritual, a high priest or priestess might direct the proceedings, just as a master of ceremonies guides a secular celebration, so everybody stays in sync. In group sex magic practices, where different people may have different response rates, energy levels, and styles—and where it's easy to get distracted—verbal directives help pace the action.

Choreographed dialogue between participants may also be part of a ritual. Just as a marriage ceremony or Christmas pageant includes spoken interactions between the people involved, magic rituals may involve sharing blessings or vows, re-enactments of mythological events, or other verbal exchanges. In sex magic rituals, as in any type of lovemaking, passionately expressed endearments can elevate the partners' excitement and increase intimacy. When you engage in ordinary sex, you might compliment your partner's breasts or penis; when you do sex magic you honor and adore your lover's body. In chapter 12, you'll find rituals that include examples of sex magic dialogue between partners.

The vibration produced in your body when you intone a word or phrase—especially one that holds meaning for you—can actually shift your personal resonance to a higher level and enhance your power. This is one reason for chanting during a ritual. We live in a world of resonance, and any sound alters that resonance. Chanting and/or singing as a group also unifies the members of the ritual while raising the energy in the magical space and within each participant.

When you state something aloud, you emphasize its importance. Like writing an idea down, saying it brings it into the physical realm. Vows, oaths, and promises are almost always uttered aloud, often in the presence of other people or deities as witnesses. Verbalizing an intention in a spell adds to its impact in a similar way. You declare your intention to yourself, your partner, your group, or the Divine. You feel a greater commitment to your goal, and a greater sense of authority. Magicians often conclude spells with a definitive statement such as "so mote it be" to seal the spell and command it to manifest.

As with all types of magic, the more emotion and energy you project into a spoken charm, the more power it has. Try infusing a verbal charm with sex energy to kick it up a notch. Choose one word or a short affirmation and shout it out at the moment of orgasm. See what happens when you make a joyful noise.

Amulets

Although the terms amulet and talisman are frequently used interchangeably, the two actually perform opposite functions. Amulets prevent something undesirable from happening. They repel evil forces, both physical and nonphysical. They shield you from illness or injury. The word amulet comes from the Latin *amuletum,* meaning "a charm"; however, amulets surely existed long before the advent of the Latin language.

You can fashion amulets to safeguard you, your family and friends, your home, business, car, or pets from circumstances or entities—known and unknown—that you consider potentially harmful. Amulets may be fixed in place, like the rowan branches our Celtic ancestors hung over their doorways and the hex signs the Pennsylvania Dutch paint on their barns. You can also wear or carry a portable amulet, such as a special crystal, a pentagram, or a medicine bag filled with substances intended to provide protection.

Ingredients for Amulets

Your belief in the amulet's protective power is what makes it work. However, plants, crystals, and other items found in nature lend their innate energies to the amulet's function. You can combine stones, shells, herbs, feathers, symbols, images, milagros, and/or other meaningful objects to reinforce the amulet's magic.

Some amulets contain several items that are carefully chosen because their resonances match your intention. Herbs and dried plant material are among the most common ingredients; the following list offers suggestions.

- *Protection:* basil, anise, burdock, comfrey, fennel, garlic, rosemary, rowan, ash, vervain, poppy seeds

- *Purification/banishing:* sage, burdock, frankincense, pine

- *Intuition/psychic ability:* bay, frankincense, mugwort, yarrow

· *Peace/relaxation:* chamomile, lavender, hops, lemongrass, vanilla

You might wish to create a special sigil, using one of the techniques described in chapter 10, and display it as an amulet. Or, draw a rune of protection on a piece of paper, dot the paper with essential oil of amber or basil, and slip the paper into an amulet pouch. If you burn a candle for the purpose of protection, save some chips of wax and add them to your amulet.

Sympathetic magic, which relies on symbolic associations, might also play a part. For example, an amulet designed to provide safety during a plane trip could include a toy airplane. One to protect you when you run the bulls at Pamplona might contain a pinch of ground-up bull's horn.

Creating an Amulet

The colors you choose for your amulet are significant as well. Magicians usually associate white and black with protection. If you use a black pouch to hold your ingredients, you could tie it with a white ribbon (or vice versa). Blend in a little knot magic by tying three knots in the ribbon and projecting your intention into the knots (see chapter 8 for more information). Once you've sealed your amulet, don't open it.

The process of creating an amulet, whether you paint an evil eye on the front door of your house or fabricate a portable charm, is a magic spell. Consequently, it's a good idea to cast a circle around the space where you fashion the amulet and smudge the area to clear it of any unwanted energies. Add an astrological advantage by preparing your amulet during the waning moon, preferably when the sun or moon is in Capricorn.

When you've finished, use sex energy to charge the amulet and activate its power (see the "elixir of love" later in this chapter for instructions). An amulet's power lasts until a situation occurs that compels it to act. Therefore, the protective energy of the amulet may remain latent for quite a while. Once drawn upon to serve its purpose, the amulet is usually exhausted and you'll have to either recharge it or acquire a new one. If you make it through the streets of Pamplona without getting gored or trampled by fellow runners, that baby's done its job and you can retire it.

Talismans

The word talisman is said to derive from the Arabic *talis ma*, which means "magical writing." In ancient times, when few people other than priests and sages were literate, writing held magical and mystical significance. Both the physical act of writing and the letters themselves were believed to impart power to an object. Today, of course, most magicians accept that the practitioner's energy, projected into the object via thoughts and emotions, gives the charm its power. However, the act of writing can contribute to the magic by helping you to focus and clarify your thinking.

Types of Talismans

A talisman's purpose is to attract something you desire: love, money, fame, good health, and so on. Like amulets, talismans can be found, handmade, purchased ready-made, or passed down to you from someone else. A talisman may be a single object, perhaps a heart-shaped stone you carry to attract a lover, or a collection of many items, such as treasure box filled with crystals, herbs, and lots of other meaningful materials. Many people favor jewelry, particularly birthstones, as talismans. Sigils, runes, astrological signs, and other symbols can serve as talismans, either individually or combined with various ingredients in a talisman pouch. My brother even had the kanji symbol for prosperity tattooed on his shoulder as a talisman to attract wealth.

Bathing can confer talismanic properties to your body. The ancient Greeks and Romans considered water to be a gift from the gods. "Taking the waters," particularly the waters of mineral-rich hot springs, has long been prized as a means for attaining good health. Soaking in scented water has obvious implications for enticing a lover and as a prelude to sex magic when your goal is to attract something you desire. A leisurely dip in a tub of magically prepared hot water soothes your emotions, elevates your personal energies, and imprints your skin with your intentions. Try some or all of the following suggestions:

- Add to your bathwater one or more essential oils that relate to your intention.

- Use soap made with herbs that relate to your intention (see the following list).

- Place crystals and/or gemstones that correspond to your intention in the bathwater.

- In your bathwater float candles that symbolize your intention.

· Infuse a glass of water with your intention by writing a word such as love or money on a piece of paper and taping it to the glass so the writing faces in. After allowing the water to absorb your intention for a few minutes, empty the glass into the tub of water.

Want a permanent talisman? Plant a tree or shrub whose meaning corresponds to your objective. Cedar trees, for example, are associated with money, apricot trees with love, ash trees with protection, and oaks with strength. If you wish, you can bury an object that symbolizes your intention, such as a coin to attract prosperity, beneath a tree. The ancient Chinese system of magic known as feng shui recommends installing lights, water features, and other intention-laden objects in specific places in your home or yard to attract health, wealth, and happiness.

Some people designate certain garments as talismans (remember those stinky socks I mentioned earlier?). Maybe you have a lucky belt or hat. Maybe your cowboy boots give you a sense of power. When you wear a sexy dress to a party in hopes of attracting a lover or a designer suit to a job interview, your outfit becomes a type of talisman. Magicians often wear special clothing for ritual purposes to enhance their energies and transport them from a mundane to a magical place.

Ingredients for Talismans

Your belief is the source of a talisman's power, but combining natural ingredients with complementary energies can aid its function. Gemstones and crystals, symbols and images, or any objects that hold meaning for you can serve as talismans. Many magicians include herbs and dried plant material in talisman pouches.

- *Love:* red clover, raspberry, catnip, cinnamon, myrtle, gentian, cocoa

- *Prosperity:* mint, cedar, cinnamon, clove, parsley

- *Career success:* clove, cinnamon, laurel, hawthorn, sandalwood, cedar, frankincense

- *Sexuality:* cayenne, ginger, curry, cumin, paprika

- *Communication:* celery seed, caraway, dill, fern, valerian, sassafras

- *Strength:* hemp, comfrey, elm, oak, moss

Creating a Talisman

If you're creating a talisman, use colors that relate to your objective—pink and red for love/passion, gold and silver for money, and so on (see chapter 9 for more information). As when fashioning amulets, you might choose a talisman pouch of one color and tie it with a ribbon of another, incorporating knot magic into the process. Before you begin, cast a circle and smudge the space where you'll do your spell.

The waxing moon, because it's associated with growth, is a good time to make a talisman. Tap astrological energies that support your intention by doing your magic when the moon is in an appropriate sign.

- *To attract love or improve a romantic relationship:* Libra, Taurus

- *To attract prosperity:* Taurus, Scorpio

- *To attract fame/recognition:* Leo
- *For career success:* Leo, Capricorn
- *For a pleasant or productive trip:* Sagittarius
- *To get a home:* Cancer
- *For vigor, courage, or athletic ability:* Aries
- *For intuition, insight, or imagination:* Pisces
- *For creativity:* Leo, Libra, Pisces
- *For matters involving intellect or communication:* Gemini
- *For general health:* Virgo
- *For friendship or group activities:* Aquarius

When you've finished fashioning your talisman, charge it to activate its power (see the "elixir of love" on page 209 for instructions). Because a talisman operates 24/7, sending out energy to attract what you desire, its lifespan probably won't be as long as an amulet's. If you haven't achieved your goal after a certain amount of time has passed, consider recharging your talisman. To boost a talisman's power, "feed" it by dabbing a little essential oil on it (some sources suggest blood). Better yet, charge it with a magical substance known as "elixir."

Fetishes, Totems, and Power Objects

Virtually any item can be imbued with magical power. The treasured object's power comes from the energy with which you invest it and the emotional connection you form with it. Magicians create and employ a variety of magical objects, for myriad purposes. Work with the ones that appeal to you and suit your objectives.

Fetishes

A fetish differs from an amulet or talisman in one significant way: its bearer believes the object is linked to a higher source. Although educated Westerners often associate fetishes with aboriginal peoples, the Catholic's rosary is a good example of a fetish.

Usually, a fetish serves only one purpose—to attract health, money, or love, not all three at once. To summon a fetish's magic, you can simply wear or carry it. Or, you can burn it to release your intentions into the universe. Some fetishes are designed to be buried, which allows your intentions to gestate and grow in the earth's fertile soil. Others can be floated on water. One summer night, a group of women friends and I performed a Brazilian *Macumba* ritual, during which we attached fetishes, flowers, and candles to a large buoyant wreath. Then we waded out fully dressed into the Atlantic Ocean to set the wreath adrift—while a confused cop in a squad car watched dutifully to make sure we didn't drown.

Totems

A totem is a personal spirit guide or guardian, usually an animal, bird, or reptile. A totem animal may exist in both the physical and nonphysical worlds, or it may be a spirit being who has never actually incarnated. Totems offer protection, healing, and guidance to individuals as well as to clans.

If you feel a special affinity with a particular creature, it might be your totem. Perhaps you even possess some of the qualities associated with your totem animal—the strength of an elephant, the speed of a cheetah, the grace of a swan. Your totem might appear to you in the flesh, or in dreams or visions. Usually it shows up to give you a message or to offer assistance. You may wish to keep a small figurine that represents your totem and display it on your altar. People in the American Southwest often wear jewelry or clothing depicting their totems. Although the object itself may have no innate power of its own, it can serve as a touchstone linking you to your spirit guardian.

Power Objects

A power object can be anything to which you attribute special significance. A memento or souvenir that reminds you of happy times and therefore raises your resonance could be a power object. So could a stone, pinecone, feather, or other item found in nature. Most likely, you've already collected a number of power objects, you just didn't call them by that name.

In some cases, a power object may physically resemble your intention. For instance, a *shiva lingam* is a smooth, elongated stone shaped rather like a penis. Frequently a ring of a different color circles the stone. Considered sacred in India, a shiva lingam symbolizes divine manifestation in the material world. For many people, this stone's phallic shape represents the god Shiva and masculine power, whereas the ring signifies the opening to the vagina, feminine energy, and the goddess Shakti. Therefore, you could use a shiva lingam as a power object to help you attract a mate, to improve a relationship, or to enhance your sexual ability.

You can carry, wear, or display a power object to assist you in working magic. If you wish, combine several power objects in a talisman, amulet, or medicine bundle.

The Elixir of Love

Until you charge an amulet or talisman, it lacks magical power. Your energy animates it. Some magicians design elaborate rituals for charging charms, but a simple "four elements" practice works just fine. First, sprinkle your amulet or talisman with saltwater and say, "I charge you with water and earth." Then hold it in the smoke of burning incense and say, "I charge you with fire and air." That's it. Your willpower does the rest.

Sex magicians, however, often prefer a different method, one that imparts a great deal more pizzazz to an amulet, talisman, or other charm. This method utilizes the creative force that abides in what's sometimes called the elixir of love. "Elixir" in this case refers to the blend of male and female sexual fluids. Your primordial goo is rich with creative potential—not only for producing babies, but for generating magical outcomes of all kinds. Don't let it go to waste.

Charging Objects with Elixir

Bring whatever objects you wish to charge into your sacred space. Keep them near you while you have sex, so they pick up the power-packed resonance of your sexual energy. After engaging in intercourse with magical intent, spend a few minutes lying together to allow the mixture of your fluids to be partly reabsorbed through the vaginal walls and the head of the penis. Then use the blend to charge charms and/or other magic tools. Your fluids contain your magical energy along with the essence of your intention. Try these applications:

- Dab a little elixir on an amulet or talisman pouch.

- Rub some on a crystal or gemstone.

- Put a drop or two on a sigil.

- Dot a power object with elixir.

- Dress a candle with elixir blended in oil.

- Anoint your pentagram, wand, chalice, and athame with it.

- If you've done knot magic, slick a bit of elixir on the knots.

Embodying Elixir

Now it's time for finger painting. Dip your finger in the elixir and use it to draw on your partner's body a sigil or other symbol that signifies your intention. Your partner does the same thing on your body. Allow the elixir to dry and become absorbed by your skin.

Next, consume some of the elixir. The simplest way is for the man to lick it from his partner's body, and then share a kiss. Contemporary women rarely have problems with this part, but some straight men do. If you're squeamish, here's an alternative you might find more palatable. Scoop up some elixir with a spoon and stir it into wine or fruit juice, and then sip the mixture from your ritual chalice. In fact, you can add elixir to any magic potion to boost the drink's potency.

Wipe up what's left with a clean cloth, such as a linen handkerchief, napkin, tea towel, or T-shirt. Any natural material will do (shun the synthetics). Save this cloth—you can cut it into pieces and add the elixir-imprinted bits to amulets, talismans, and medicine bags in the future. You can also burn the cloth in a ritual fire.

Obviously, this technique is designed for healthy, heterosexual couples.

- If you and your primary magical partner are of the same sex, you'll have to bring in someone of the opposite gender to produce an elixir that contains both male and female juices. This is a good opportunity for a *ménage à trois.*

- If you're using a condom for contraceptive purposes, you'll have to do *in vitro* blending.

- If one (or both) of you has a STD, scrap the whole idea.

Charging Charms in a Group Ritual

If you wish, you can work with a group to charge talismans, amulets, and other charms. By combining your collective energy you increase a spell's power exponentially. The spell may be performed for one person, the whole group, humankind in general, or for any purpose you agree on. Do the usual smudging, circle-casting, and banishing rituals. Sit or lie in a circle, and place the charm in the center, where everyone can see it easily. You may charge more than one object simultaneously; however, all charms should be created for the same telos.

Let's say, for example, you've decided as a group to do sex magic to bring peace to your community. You could lay a string of prayer flags in the center of your circle. In addition, you might place a talisman there that includes herbs, gemstones, sigils, and other ingredients related to harmony and protection, contained in a wooden box.

Begin the process of arousal, using whatever methods and pairings you've deemed appropriate for this ritual. Your circle should include both sexes, however, in order to produce a magical elixir. Upon determining that the resonance is high enough, the group's leader directs everyone to look at the objects and send energy toward them. As members of the group engage in sex, keep your intention in mind. During orgasm (which may, but probably won't, happen simultaneously), focus on your telos and release your energy into the matrix.

After resting for a bit, collect the elixir generated by the various members of the group and blend it together. Dot some on each prayer flag and on the wooden box. Mix the rest with wine, fruit juice, or spring water in a chalice and share the beverage, saving some for later.

When you feel ready, take the prayer flags outside and hang them where the wind will cause them to flutter. The breeze carries your intentions throughout your community. Next, bury the box near a tree or body of water. Pour the rest of the elixir-imprinted wine, juice, or water on the ground to nurture your talisman and telos.

Manifestation Books, Cards, and Boxes

More than a decade ago, my friend Lyndsey Powers and I started keeping "manifestation books." We discovered that our intentions materialized faster and more effectively if we wrote them down, instead of just holding them in our thoughts. The act of writing focuses your ideas and brings your intentions one step closer to the physical world. Writing engages your imagination. Furthermore, holding a pen activates acupressure points in your fingers and sends electronic cues to your brain: *Get busy and make this happen now.*

Manifestation books, cards, and boxes incorporate some of the techniques we've discussed earlier: pictures, written words, symbols, and so on. These tools continue to remind you of your objectives. They also incubate your intentions, and nurture them into manifestation.

Manifestation Books

Your manifestation book could be a bound journal in which you describe, in detail, what you intend to attract into your life. However, Lyndsey and I prefer a three-ring binder with dividers for different categories such as money, relationships, career goals, home, health, travel, and so on. A three-ring binder also allows you to continue updating your book, adding and removing pages as necessary.

Use a separate sheet of paper for each intention. State your objective as an affirmation—a positive statement written in the present tense, as if the condition already exists. For example: *I now have more than enough money for everything I need and desire.* Describe your objective in as much detail as you can. Generally speaking, specificity is a good thing and enables you to attract exactly what you want, rather than just something close. If you're manifesting a new computer, car, or sound system, state the model and features you want.

What if you aren't privy to the specifics? In this case you'll have to rely on your inner knowing and/or a higher power to bring to you what's right for you. As Dr. Wayne Dyer says in *The Power of Intention,* "Create a knowing within, and let the universal mind of intention handle the details."

End your statement with the words "this or something better" to make sure you aren't limiting yourself and your options. Expect opportunities to show up and be open to all types of opportunities. Most of us think too small. Consequently, we settle for life circumstances that are less satisfactory, less joyful, and less vibrant than we could have had if we'd widened our field of vision. The universe can come up with many more ways to fulfill your dreams than you might have imagined by yourself.

Combine visual imagery with writing. Draw pictures, symbols, sigils, and/or other images that represent your intentions. Cut out magazine photos and paste them onto the pages of your book. Download images from the Internet. Use colored paper if you like and decorate the sheets in any way that you find appealing.

Keep your book nearby when you engage in sex magic to infuse it with your high-octane energy. Charge each page magically. My preference is to dab elixir on all four corners, but you can use essential oils, saltwater, candle wax, or another method if you'd rather.

Read through your manifestation book regularly— every morning and every night before you go to bed, if possible. This practice keeps your intentions in the forefront of your mind and reinforces your belief. Indulge your imagination; feel the pleasure of having your wishes come true.

Revise, expand, and fine-tune your objectives as need be. In your manifestation book, express gratitude for all the good things that come your way. When one of your intentions materializes, write your thanks in your book. As you do, you pave the way to receive more opportunities and more blessings. Your confidence grows and you open yourself to the infinite abundance the universe has to give you.

Vision Cards

I also like to make cards that visually convey my intentions. First, I cut four-by-six-inch or five-by-seven-inch rectangles from poster board. Then I cut out magazine pictures and words that describe my goals, and glue them to the card blanks. Each card expresses one intention only. Although similar to a vision board, the small size allows me to hone my focus more precisely. I can carry a card or two with me in my purse or pocket, or prop one up on my altar, desk, or bedside table. I gaze at the cards frequently to engage my imagination and fortify my belief that the desired outcome is on its way to me.

My manifestation cards have produced interesting and sometimes unexpected results. In September of 2009, for instance, I created a card that featured a picture of a woman holding two fiery torches. To me she represented creative power. About a week later, I attended a women's retreat in Texas. There I learned about the art of poi spinning, or twirling fire, which I'd never heard of before but which turned out to be an incredibly empowering experience. (You can see my card and photo and read a description of the experience on my blog, www.magickmurdersex .blogspot.com.)

Charge your cards with elixir (or another method), as you would any other tool to activate it. Bring your cards into your sacred space when you perform sex magic, so they can absorb your energy. At the moment of orgasm, you can look at a vision card just as you would a tarot card to project your telos into the universe.

Manifestation Boxes

Manifestation boxes serve a similar purpose. However, this tool emphasizes allowing instead of action, that is, turning your wishes over to the universe to handle. Allowing is the second, and equally vital, part of manifestation. Once you've launched your intention, you must allow the universe to bring it to fruition.

Acquire a box you find attractive, such as an antique jewelry box. Or, make your own manifestation box from a shoebox, decorating it with pictures, symbols, affirmations, and other adornments that hold meaning for you. On slips of paper, write your intentions. Use colors that relate to your objectives.

Fold each slip of paper and charge it by dabbing elixir on the paper (or another substance if you prefer). Envision your wishes materializing. Imagine you are letting go and handing over responsibility for manifesting these requests to the universe. Feel a sense of serenity, confidence, and well-being. Place the slips of paper in the box and put the lid on. As you do, you relinquish control and trust that your intentions will be fulfilled in the right way, at the right time.

Add requests as often as you like. When a wish comes true, remove from the box the slip of paper on which you'd written that intention and burn the paper. Express gratitude for the blessings you've received. I often express gratitude by making a donation to a charity or by doing a good deed for someone else—this seems to help keep the flow of abundance circling through the universe and brings more abundance back to me.

Rites and Rituals

Our daily lives are comprised of rituals of many kinds, from that first cup of coffee in the morning to that last trip to the bathroom before retiring for the night. Rituals help us establish order in our lives. They enable us to break down the vastness of human existence into manageable segments. The uncertainty of the future can, at times, seem a bit frightening and overwhelming, but familiar rituals give us a sense of security.

Through ritualized rites we mark the passage of time. Holiday celebrations, birthdays and anniversaries, school graduations, weddings, retirement parties, and funerals anchor us in time and provide continuity in our lives. Like road signs, they serve as guides and markers on the journey.

All cultures and spiritual traditions enact rituals. Every piece of a ritual—the space where it takes place, the words spoken, the participants' movements, clothing, music, decorations, food and drink—contributes to the ambiance and the ritual's purpose. The same holds true in magical rituals.

Some rituals are primarily celebratory in nature. Others are designed to produce a specific outcome or to evoke a certain state of awareness in the minds of the participants. The steps of the ritual focus your thoughts and raise energy. If the ritual involves a group of people, it also unites the members and joins their individual energies toward a mutual goal. A good ritual transports you from the mundane into the magical realm, where all things become possible.

Ritual Baths

In preparation for spellworking, ceremonies, and rites, magicians often take ritual baths to remove unwanted energies so they can enter sacred space in a pure, receptive state. When you're doing sex magic, it's nice to smell fresh and clean when you meet your partner, too. Bathe with your partner or alone, whichever you prefer.

Create a Magical Ambiance

Turn out the lights and illuminate the bathroom with candles. Play music that sets the tone for your spellworking and seduction. Position crystals on the sides of the tub, or immerse them in the bathwater. Let yourself unwind and release all thoughts that don't pertain to your magical objective. Sprinkle some sea salt into the bathwater for the purpose of purification. Then, if you like, add several drops of an essential oil that relates to your intention:

- *Love:* rose, patchouli, ylang-ylang, jasmine, musk

- *Prosperity:* peppermint, cedar, clove, cinnamon

- *Career success:* sandalwood, frankincense, clove

- *Protection:* amber, rosemary, fennel, basil

- *Purification:* pine, camphor, eucalyptus, sage

- *Relaxation/serenity:* lavender, chamomile, clary sage, marjoram

- *Happiness/well-being:* bergamot, orange blossom, gentian, melissa

Preparing Yourself for Sex Magic

Bathing literally steeps you in the element of water, which metaphysicians associate with the emotions, intuition, and creativity—the aspects of yourself that you want to heighten when doing magic. As you soak in preparation for your magical work, allow your awareness to shift from a reliance on everyday rational, logical thinking to that of imagination and feeling.

Let the warm water relax and tantalize you. Allow the exotic scents of jasmine, patchouli, or ylang-ylang to awaken your libido. If you're bathing with a partner in preparation for sex magic, soap each other and begin fore-play in the bath. Whirlpool tub jets and hand-held show-erheads offer all sorts of erotic possibilities. Take your time and luxuriate in this first stage of your ritual.

If you and your partner have opted to bathe separately, you can still begin the process of arousal while immersed in your ritual bath. This is the time to indulge your fantasies and imagine your objectives materializing. When you're ready to meet, dress in loose-fitting robes made of silk or another sensual material. All your senses are heightened as you enter your sacred space in a state of anticipatory bliss.

Circle Casting and Banishing

Regardless of how simple or complex a spell, magicians usually begin with the ritual of circle casting and banishing. This practice prepares your mind for working magic, centers you in magical space, and connects you to the cosmic forces that will assist your efforts. If you've done any kind of intentional magic you probably know how to cast a circle, but I'll include a few options here just in case.

Preparing to Cast a Circle

Casting a circle around the area where you'll be working serves two purposes: it keeps unwanted energies out of your sacred space, and it contains the energies you raise during the spell until you're ready to release them. A circle may be physical or nonphysical, or both. You can use a quick and easy method, such as envisioning yourself and your sacred space surrounded by white light, or perform an intricate and multilayered ritual. You can draw a temporary circle in the sand on the beach that the incoming tide will wash away, or create a permanent circle that will last for centuries, like the ancient stone circles at Stonehenge and Avebury, England.

Before you cast the circle, clear unwanted energies from your magical space. You can smudge the space by burning sage and wafting the smoke around the area. Or, sprinkle the space with salt or saltwater. Some magicians slice the air with an athame or sword to cut away energetic imbalances and disruptive forces. Wiccans sometimes sweep the area with brooms. Use whatever method(s) you prefer to purify your sacred space and ready it for your ritual.

Just in case this isn't obvious, I'll mention it: remove any physical clutter, dirt, and junk from your magical space. Unless something plays a role in your ritual or in some way enriches your experience, it doesn't belong there. Any objects you bring into your sacred space should be smudged or cleansed beforehand, too.

The Lesser Banishing Ritual of the Pentagram: A Variation

If I'm in a hurry, I simply visualize myself enclosed in a circle of white light. When I'm going to perform a longer spell, ritual, or ceremony, however, I usually prefer the simplified variation of the Lesser Banishing Ritual of the Pentagram, described below. (I direct you to Donald Michael Kraig's *Modern Sex Magic* if you want to learn how to do the complete LBRP.)

1. Begin by standing at the middle of the area where you'll be working. Close your eyes and take a few slow, deep breaths to calm and center your mind. Then envision the space around you glowing with white light and say, "This sacred space is now cleared of all harmful, disruptive, and unbalanced energies; it is filled with divine white light and love."

2. Next, extend your right arm above your head and draw down a beam of white light. Visualize

it running through your body, from your head to your feet, and into the ground. Then hold your arms outstretched at your sides, parallel to the ground. Imagine a beam of white light crossing your body, extending from fingertips to fingertips and beyond as you say, "As above, so below. As within, so without."

3. After opening your eyes, go to the easternmost point of your sacred space. Use your athame to draw a pentagram in the air before you. (If you don't have an athame, you can use your finger.) Holding your athame, walk clockwise and trace an arc in the air with it until you reach the south. There draw another pentagram in the air. Continue walking clockwise, extending the arc to the west, where you'll draw a third pentagram. Then move to the north, draw the last pentagram, and complete the circle by returning to the east, so that you are now enclosed within the circle.

4. Stand in the center of the circle, facing east. Hold your arms outstretched at your sides and position your feet about shoulder-width apart. Envision blue light flowing through your legs, arms, and head, crossing your body and illuminating you as a human pentagram, while you say, "About me shines the five-pointed star."

5. If you like, you can now call in guardians, guides, angels, et cetera to protect and assist you in your ritual. For example, say, "Before me Raphael, angel of air, guardian of the east, please guide and protect, bless and empower me. Behind me Gabriel, angel of water, guardian of the west, please guide

and protect, bless and empower me. To my right Michael, angel of fire, guardian of the south, please guide and protect, bless and empower me. To my left Uriel, angel of earth, guardian of the north, please guide and protect, bless and empower me."

6. If you prefer, you can summon the beings known as Wards or Watchtowers, who guard the four directions, by chanting: "Guardian of the eastern sphere/now I seek your presence here/come, east, come/be here this night (day)." Face the direction as you speak. Continue in this manner to call upon the Wards of the south, west, and north.

7. Sometimes I ring a bell or play a singing bowl at this stage to mark the completion of this step, before progressing to my spell or ritual. I usually light incense and candles, too. Do whatever feels right to you.

8. After completing your spell or ritual, open the circle and release whatever beings you may have invited to join you in your sacred space. For example, go to the east, point your athame at the place where you drew the first pentagram, and say, "Thank you Raphael. Hail, farewell, and blessed be." Holding your athame pointing outward, retrace your earlier steps in reverse order by walking counterclockwise to the north. When you arrive there say, "Thank you Uriel. Hail, farewell, and blessed be." Go to the west, then to the south, and repeat this parting statement to Gabriel and Michael. Or, if you've called in the Wards/Watchtowers of the four directions, say, "Hail East, thanks, farewell, and blessed be," and so on to release these Wards.

9. Now that the circle is open, the energy you've raised and the magic you've performed can flow out into the universe—and you can return to your everyday world.

Circle Casting with the Four Elements

Another simpler technique involves lighting a stick of incense and walking around the circle, starting at the east and moving clockwise. As you trail smoke behind you, say, "With fire and air I cast this magic circle." Next, sprinkle saltwater on the ground, again starting in the east, and as you walk clockwise around the circle say, "With water and earth I cast this magic circle."

If you're working with a partner, cast the circle together. The man draws the circle with the burning incense (fire and air are masculine elements) while the woman casts with saltwater (water and earth are feminine elements). Same-sex partners can choose whichever elements you prefer.

You'll find lots of information about circle casting and banishing online and in other books about magic. You can also design your own ritual. Some magicians hold firmly to established guidelines, but I believe a ritual can be more powerful and meaningful if you personalize it so it suits your temperament and purposes. Whatever method you choose, enact it with confidence, enthusiasm, and flair.

Circles for Sex Magic

Because I consider ambiance especially important in sex magic rituals, I like to cast a circle that's not only effective, but visually appealing as well. Often I circle the bed or area where I'll be working with candles. Sometimes I choose candles of a color that relates to my intention; other times I include all the colors of the rainbow. Beginning in the east, I light the candles one at a time while moving in a clockwise direction. To open the circle after completing the magic ritual, I snuff out the candles in reverse order.

Candles scented with essential oils engage your sense of smell, the sense most closely linked with erotic feelings. In his novel *Jitterbug Perfume,* Tom Robbins writes delightfully about the connection between scent, sex, and magic: "Perfume is the medium by which the lady magically usurps the sexual powers of the blossom … the perfumer is dealing in sexual magic."

Sometimes I circle my sacred space with flowers or plants that correspond to my telos. Consider surrounding the area with crystals, too, to provide protection and amplify the energy you raise during your ritual. The crystals will store the sex energy for future use as well. If you're working outdoors, a grove of trees or a ring of stones can create a natural circle.

Once all participants have entered the circle, no one should leave unless it's absolutely necessary, until you've finished the ritual. If you must leave, cut a doorway in the perimeter using your hand or athame, then step through. Seal the opening afterwards by redrawing the doorway in reverse order.

Banishing After a Ritual

After you've finished your ritual and opened the circle, perform another banishing to disperse any entities who have been drawn to your magical energy and still hover at the outskirts of your sacred space. You can simply go to each of the four directions and order these entities to leave by saying, "All beings attracted to this magic space depart now. Return home, harming none, and let there be peace between us." If you like, push them away with your hands as well.

You could use a broom to sweep the air within your ritual space and chase away any remaining entities. Or, smudge the area again with burning sage. Spritz the air with a mixture of water, salt, and pine or eucalyptus essential oil, if you'd rather. Sometimes I ring bells or chimes to break up unwanted energies or drum to clear the space. Use whatever method you prefer. As you do your banishing, envision the area filled with white light and purified.

Communing with Deities

Need some extra "spiritual muscle" to address an important matter that seems too big to handle by yourself? Maybe it's time to petition a deity for assistance. You can call upon a god, goddess, spirit guide, angel, or other entity—whatever your objective, there's someone in the spirit realm who can help you. Before you begin, determine which deity can best aid your purpose. Each has his or her own unique characteristics, powers, and areas of influence. In chapter 6, I provided a short list of gods and goddesses from various cultures. I urge you to do your homework to familiarize yourself with these and other deities, to understand their specialties and the subtleties of their personalities and powers.

Generally speaking, it's best to call upon a deity with whom you feel a connection. Because I'm of Celtic lineage, I feel an affinity with Brigid and Ceridwin. However, I also work with Kuan Yin a lot because I respect many Buddhist ideas, and with Bast because my totem animal is the cat. Be as specific as possible in your choice of deities—Apollo and Odin are both associated with poetry, for instance, but the gods are quite different in nature and one might be better suited to your purposes than the other.

If you choose to work with your totem animal, his/her assistance could be beneficial in any type of ritual. You might also ask your totem animal to bring along another spirit animal, if necessary, who specializes in things related to your particular objective at this time.

Preparing to Contact a Deity

Once you've determined who's the best guy or gal for the job, acquire an image of that deity. This could be a painting, a sculpture or figurine, an engraving, or a picture you download from the Internet. *National Geographic* is a good source for photos of animals that can signify your totem.

Before you proceed to summon the deity, dismantle all your defenses. Many magicians install protective devices, physical and nonphysical, in and around their homes and sacred spaces. These defenses, however, may prevent a deity from getting through to you. This is one time you *don't* want to cast a circle or wear your pentagram.

Clear the space where you'll be working using whatever method you prefer. You might also want to take a ritual bath.

Place the depiction of the god or goddess on your altar. You can either set up a special altar dedicated to the deity (a temporary altar is okay) or clean off the altar you normally use and only place objects on it that relate to the deity you wish to contact.

Next, offer a gift to the deity. Buddhists burn incense to summon the Buddha, and you can do the same as an invitation to your deity of choice. You could put a gift of flowers on your altar—do a little research to find out if the deity has a favorite plant or posy (see chapter 9 for some suggestions). Some offerings might be especially appropriate to give to a certain god or goddess. Bacchus, for instance, enjoys his wine, so you could set a glass of vino on your altar to appeal to him. Sprinkle a little catnip for Bast. Light a candle for Brigid, who's also known as Bright One and Lady of the Flame.

Summoning a Deity

When you're ready to communicate with the deity, sit, stand, or kneel in a comfortable position before the altar. Be respectful and sincere. Close your eyes, relax, and quiet your mind. If you know how to meditate, do so now.

When you feel calm and centered, open your eyes and gaze at the image of the deity you wish to contact. Keep your heart and mind open. Become aware of your own energy surrounding you and flowing through you. Visualize your aura expanding and growing brighter. Once you've raised your resonance to the highest level you can achieve at this time, project your energy through the image to the deity. Intend and believe that you will make a connection with the deity. Feel your energy flowing from your heart chakra out toward the spirit realm. If you wish, you can embed requests, questions, or other thoughts in the energy, in the form of words, pictures, or emotions.

Before long, if you've made contact, you should feel energy returning to you from the deity. This energy can be pretty intense, but I've always experienced it as pleasant and empowering. The energy will likely be imbued with the particular qualities of the deity you've chosen. If you're communing with Kuan Yin, you may sense boundless compassion and unconditional love coming to you. If you've connected with Brigid, you might feel inspired and enthusiastic. Bast's energy is playful and lighthearted (or at least that's how I sense it). Each deity is different.

Ask the deity how you should use his or her energy to address your intention. You'll sense a response that instructs you. You may also receive insights, guidance, or answers to questions, although this might not happen immediately. Sometimes the information works its way slowly to the surface of your consciousness.

Keep the communication going, sending and receiving energy, creating a cycle between yourself and the deity. Continue for as long as you like. When you're ready to stop, thank the god or goddess for assisting you. Hold onto the deity's energy—don't ground it. Utilize it as the deity has instructed. Allow the energy to evolve as it will, until eventually it leaves your system.

Tips for Communicating with Deities

Here are a few additional tips to keep in mind if you decide to summon a deity, paraphrased from *Rob's Magick Blog*, with permission from the author, Robert A. Peregrine:

- Don't do this before bedtime—you'll be wired for quite a while.

- Not all spirit entities are gods, and not everything listed as a "god" is actually a god. It's okay to ask deities to prove themselves, using their own methods.

- Usually deities don't mind if you ask questions, so if you don't understand something, ask.

- If you want a deity to bless an object, have it ready and request the deity's blessing during your period of communion.

- One of the worst things you can do is utilize a deity's energy for a purpose for which you don't have permission—ask first and respect the deity's wishes.

Working with Elementals

In some circumstances, you might want to seek the aid of an elemental or other being who occupies a lower rung on the spiritual ladder. Elementals are nature spirits who operate within the sphere of their element. Within that element they can be most helpful, but their areas of influence are limited. Most of the time, elementals remain invisible; however, sensitive individuals may see them, and tales of these beings abound in folklore.

- *Sylphs:* air spirits who operate in the realm of ideas and communication

- *Gnomes:* earth spirits who understand the material world and physical resources

- *Salamanders:* fire spirits whose qualities include passion, inspiration, and initiative

· *Undines:* water spirits who function in the field of emotions, imagination, and intuition

Although elementals can be useful in certain circumstances, they're not always reliable—and sometimes they're mischievous or downright malevolent. As a result, you may want to stick with higher-level spirits, at least until you've got some experience under your magical belt. If you do choose to work with them, treat these folks with respect and offer them gifts to show your appreciation. (Nancy Watson's *Practical Solitary Magic* contains some good advice for working with elementals.)

The Five-Fold Kiss

In this ritual, the members of a couple honor and bestow blessings on one another. The first and more familiar version is an enactment of reverence and greeting, which may precede a ceremony or rite such as a handfasting. Participants may be clothed or skyclad (nude), depending on the situation and their preferences. You can find this ritual described in *A Witch's Bible*, by Janet and Stewart Farrar, and elsewhere.

The second, more intimate and sensual version is one I've adapted for the practice of sex magic. It also honors and blesses the participants prior to engaging in sex. The couple must be skyclad for this ritual (or wear loose-fitting robes that can easily be opened).

Before beginning, prepare your sacred space according to the purpose of your ritual or ceremony. Take a ritual bath, either together or separately. Cast a circle, do appropriate smudging/banishing, call in deities/guardians, and so on.

Standard Version

1. The woman stands, while the man kneels before her and says: "Blessed be thy feet, that have brought thee in these ways." He kisses her right foot, and then her left.

2. He then says: "Blessed be thy knees, that shall kneel at the sacred altar." He kisses her right knee, and then her left.

3. Next he says: "Blessed be thy womb, without which we would not be." He kisses her lower belly.

4. Standing, he says: "Blessed be thy breasts, formed in beauty." He kisses her breasts, first the right one, then the left.

5. Finally, he says: "Blessed be thy lips, that shall utter the Sacred Names." He kisses her on the lips as they embrace.

Now the woman gives the blessing to the man. While he stands, she kneels before him and repeats the words and gestures. In step 3, instead of "womb" she says "phallus," "penis," or "manhood," before kissing his lower abdomen. In step 4, instead of "formed in beauty" she says "formed in strength." Some couples prefer to say "chest" here rather than "breasts."

Sex Magic Version

Before beginning, agree on a telos, and together create a sigil or select another visual that encapsulates your telos. Prepare your ritual space to reflect your intention and display your visual(s). Bring your chalice into your sacred space, along with some wine (or another beverage) to share at the conclusion of the ritual. Cast a circle and do the usual smudging/banishing, and so on.

1. The woman stands, while the man kneels before her and says: "Blessed be your feet, for they have brought you to me." He kisses her right foot, and then her left.

2. Next, he says: "Blessed be the entrance to your womanhood, which brings forth life into the world and gives me the most elegant pleasure." He kisses and tongues her clitoris and vagina.

3. Then he says: "Blessed be your womb, the source of creation without which human life would not exist." He kisses her lovingly on the lower belly.

4. Standing, he says: "Blessed be your breasts, which nurture future generations." He sucks her right nipple first, and then her left.

5. Finally, he says: "Blessed be your lips, which speak lovingly to me and give me great joy." He kisses her deeply and passionately, in a full-body embrace.

The woman now returns the blessing.

1. Kneeling before the man while he stands, she says: "Blessed be your feet, for they have brought you to me." She kisses his right foot, and then his left.

2. Next, she says: "Blessed be your manhood, which plants the seeds for future generations and gives me the most exquisite pleasure." She takes his penis into her mouth, licking and sucking it.

3. Then she says: "Blessed be the source of your seed, without which human life would not exist." She kisses his right testicle, and then his left.

4. Standing, she says: "Blessed be your heart, the center of love and life." She kisses him at the heart chakra, in the center of his chest.

5. Finally, she says: "Blessed be your lips, which speak lovingly to me and give me great joy." She kisses him deeply and passionately, in a full-body embrace.

Proceed with arousal and lovemaking, according to your preferences. As in all sex magic rituals, prolong the enjoyment for as long as is possible and comfortable for you in order to heighten your pleasure and your power. Engage in stimulation until you almost reach orgasm, then back off and allow the intensity to diminish somewhat. Repeat this at least three times (nine times is optimal).

When you're ready, focus on your telos and look at the visual image you've chosen to depict it. Then release the full force of your orgasm. As you come, either together or individually, send your creative energy through the image, into the matrix, so the universe can manifest your intention. If you wish, you can incorporate other practices, such as tying knots or charging charms.

Afterward, lie together for a while to let your fluids mingle. Then pour the beverage into your chalice and add some of the elixir of love to it. Share the drink together.

Drawing Down the Moon

The term "drawing down the moon" means invoking the power of the Divine Feminine into yourself. Although we usually associate goddess energy with women, a man can connect with a female deity and balance his feminine side by drawing down the moon into himself. The complement to this practice, known as "drawing down the sun," invites the Divine Masculine into your body. The description I offer here refers to a male-female couple invoking a goddess into the woman's body, but you can adapt the ritual to suit your own situation, intentions, and sexual preferences. The ritual for drawing down the sun is essentially the same, except the woman invokes the god into the man's body instead.

Preparing for the Ritual

Perform this ritual during the full moon, outside if weather and other circumstances permit. If you choose to wear clothing, loose-fitting garments of silver, white, or cream-colored silk are ideal. Skyclad is appropriate, too.

Choose a goddess you wish to summon and set up your altar to attract and honor Her. (If you like, refer to the list provided in chapter 6.) Try to position the altar so moonlight illuminates it. You may wish to erect a temporary altar outside if moonlight can't find its way into your home. Light some creamy-white or silver candles. Place flowers related to the moon on the altar: jasmine, gardenias, pale yellow irises, white or cream-colored roses, or water lilies. Also on the altar position an image of the goddess you wish to invoke. Typically we associate Artemis and Diana with the moon, but you can call upon any deity you want to assist you. Some sources recommend calling upon a single, specific deity, rather than "the Goddess" or "the God," but I leave that up to you.

Invoking the Goddess

After following the usual preparatory steps, greet your partner in your sacred space. You may wish to use a salutation such as "Blessed be" or "Namasté" (which means "I honor the Divine within you"), and then bless one another with the Five-Fold Kiss. If possible, stand so the moon's light falls on your bodies.

Look up at the moon together and sense the presence of the Divine Feminine. The woman spreads her arms wide, as if to embrace the moon. As she does, she sets her ego and her everyday consciousness aside, allowing her mind to grow still and blank (as in a meditative trance). The man calls to the chosen goddess by name and invites Her to enter the woman's body, summoning Her with passion and joy. He can use the following chant or another of his own design:

> "Mother of creation,
> Goddess of mystery, secrets, and wisdom,
> Queen of the heavens whose light
> illuminates even the darkest night,
> I invoke you now and invite you to
> fill this woman, your daughter,
> with your presence, love, light, and power."

The woman feels the essence of the goddess streaming down from the moon and flowing into her body. She might sense goddess energy descending upon her, gently pouring down into the crown chakra at the top of her head and spreading out through her chest, arms, belly, hips, legs, and feet. A pleasant, tingling sensation may begin glowing within her, enlivening and empowering her.

When she feels the goddess inhabiting her, she proclaims herself to be the earthly representation of the goddess by uttering the following chant. (If you prefer, use the longer and more eloquent version of this call presented on www.hecatescauldron.com, or write your own script.)

> "I am [name of goddess],
> and likewise the embodiment
> of the tri-part Goddess:
> Maiden, mother, and crone,
> Mistress and ruler of the night,
> Keeper of mysteries and magic.
> My body is a sacred temple,
> the source of life and creation.
> I am boundless and eternal,
> Present everywhere, in everything,
> All ways and always."

When the man feels confident that the goddess has entered the woman's body, he addresses her as the deity (which she now is) and kneels facing Her. He worships and adores the goddess before him with words, kisses, caresses, or whatever he believes will please the deity who now occupies his partner's body. You may then proceed to enact the Great Rite.

If you prefer, you can draw down the moon and the sun together, each of you invoking a deity into your body. Rephrase the invocation to the sun/god so it's appropriate for a male deity. As Donald Michael Kraig points out in *Modern Sex Magic*, it's a good idea to familiarize yourself beforehand with the deities you are petitioning to be sure they're *simpatico*. Deities whose natures aren't innately compatible might not function together amicably in your bodies or work with you harmoniously in your ritual.

The Great Rite

For us humans, making love with a god or goddess is, to put it mildly, a heavenly experience. We have to assume the deities like it, too, if they opt to enact the rite with us. Deities, of course, don't have physical bodies, thus they can only delight in the sensation of sex by temporarily slipping on the human forms of willing participants. The eighteenth-century Hasidic master Reb Hayim Haikel proposed that we actually chose to incarnate as human beings so we could enjoy sex.

The primary reason for performing the Great Rite is to enter into deep, intimate contact with the Divine. However, during this rite you may also request a favor or gift from the deity. If this is your intention, create a sigil or other visual before beginning the rite. The image should symbolically express your intention. Place this image where you can see it easily during the rite. The deity who inhabits your body, because He or She is one with you at the time, will comprehend the meaning of the symbol.

Enacting the Rite

After you've invited the God and/or Goddess into you, using the ritual for drawing down the sun/moon, gently remove each other's clothing (if any). Gaze upon one another with love and reverence. Express your love and devotion to one another, in whatever ways please you—remember, your partner is the human embodiment of the Divine, and you are uniting not with another person, but with the god or goddess. "Unless you see someone or something in the light of love, you do not see them at all," writes Sirona Knight in *Love, Sex, and Magick.*

If you like, you can anoint your bodies with scented oils. Proceed to arouse each other in whatever ways excite you. Take your time. Prolong the pleasure as you would in any sex magic ritual. Allow the energy to build slowly and engage your sensual feelings fully, heightening your power along with your pleasure.

You'll probably notice that making love with a deity has a different quality than sex with a mere moral. The feeling may be more intense, blissful, or something else. (If, for any reason, it becomes uncomfortable for you, use your will to disperse the deity and regain possession of your body.)

Continue for as long as you like. When you finally reach climax, savor the joyful connection you've made with the deity and allow yourself to embrace the heights of resplendent pleasure. If you've established a telos and created a visual image beforehand that depicts your intention, gaze at the image now and sense the God or Goddess fulfilling your request.

After Completing the Rite

After you've finished, thank the deity or deities for joining you in this rite and for honoring you with their presence. If you've asked for a favor or blessing, thank them for their generosity and assistance in manifesting your request. Infusing your telos with the energy of a god and/or goddess can greatly enhance its power. After a while, the god/goddess will depart, and you'll know that your rite is concluded.

When you're ready, consume your elixir, imprinted with divine energy, either blended in a beverage or "neat." You can also use it to charge charms or magical tools (as described in chapter 11). End the ritual with a banishment to disperse any unwanted spirits who may have been attracted by the energy you've raised during the rite.

Some people have trouble distinguishing between a human partner and the God or Goddess within. Although it may be ideal to honor the divine nature within everyone, try not to confuse the person with the deity after you've finished this rite. If you and your partner are already a couple in the mundane world, performing the Great Rite together can enrich your appreciation of one another, deepen your intimacy, and strengthen your relationship in countless ways. However, if your partner is not your mate, you may invite confusion or disappointment if you attempt to extend the blissful feelings you've experienced beyond the limits of the rite.

Timing Rituals and Spells

Timing may not be everything in magic, but it helps. For every reason, there's a season. Many magicians—Wiccans and other Pagans in particular—like to perform rituals and spells on the eight sabbats or Great Days. These holidays, rooted in the pre-Christian cultures of Europe, Britain, and

Ireland, commemorate nature's annual cycle of life, death, and rebirth. Therefore, the rituals associated with the sabbats usually emphasize the qualities of the seasons: planting seeds in springtime, rejoicing in the fruitfulness of summer, harvesting nature's bounty in autumn, retreating and turning inward in winter.

The Eight Sabbats

The sabbats are based on the sun's movement through the zodiac. The Solstices and Equinoxes occur when the sun reaches 0 degrees of the cardinal signs Aries, Cancer, Libra, and Capricorn. The other four holidays, known as the cross-quarter days, are generally celebrated as follows, when the sun occupies the fixed signs Taurus, Leo, Scorpio, and Aquarius. You can draw upon the elevated energy present during these "power days" to enhance whatever magic you choose to do.

- *Samhain (All Hallow's Eve), October 31:* a time for honoring loved ones who have departed the earth, it's also the witches' New Year's Eve and supports new beginnings. This is a good time to perform spells to attract new things into your life, such as a new job, new romance, new home, et cetera, or to change things about yourself that you don't like. Many magicians like to do divination or to communicate with nonphysical entities during Samhain because the veil between the worlds is thinnest on this night.

- *Yule (Winter Solstice), around December 21:* a time of renewal, joy, and promise, it marks the shortest day of the year and celebrates life during the harshness of winter. During this time of incubation, I like to do spells that support slow, steady growth. If you're engaged in a long-term project or undertaking that will require perseverance, such as building a business or getting a college degree, tapping Yule's energy could benefit you.

· *Brigid's Day (Imbolc, Candlemas), February 1:* a time of creativity and inspiration, it affirms life as the days continue to lengthen. Let the Celtic goddess Brigid lend her energy to spells that involve creativity of any kind. This is the perfect day for painters, musicians, writers, and other artists to work magic. Imbolc means "in the belly" so if your goal is to get pregnant, do sex magic on this sabbat.

· *Ostara (Spring Equinox), around March 20–21:* this first day of spring is the time to plant seeds, literally and figuratively. Do magic to foster new beginnings on this sabbat. Whether you wish to begin a new job or business venture, a new relationship, a course of study, or a journey, Ostara's energy can help you jump-start your intention.

· *Beltane, May 1:* this holiday of fertility celebrates sexuality and creativity of all kinds. Like Brigid's Day, this is a good time to do magic for creative purposes—not just in the artistic sense, but to conceive, nurture, or birth any project. Do prosperity spells and love spells now. The fertile energy of Beltane might also help you conceive a child— traditionally, children conceived on this holiday were said to belong to the Goddess.

· *Midsummer (Summer Solstice), around July 21–23:* a time of fullness, it's the season to enjoy the earth's abundance. The summer's peak brings endeavors to fruition. On this day, do magic to reap the rewards of your efforts. This is also a good time to do spells for success or to make a favorable impression on others. Consider scrying now, especially if you want to discover something that's been hidden from you or to see what the future holds.

· *Lughnassadh (Lammas), August 1:* the first "waning" festival, it marks the advent of the harvest season and recognizes the sun's declining power. Like all waning periods, Lughnassadh is a time for spells that involve decrease. If you want to cut expenses, lose weight, or end a bad habit, this sabbat's energy can help you.

· *Mabon (Fall Equinox), around September 21–22:* this festival celebrates the harvest and looks ahead to a time of rest and withdrawal as colder weather approaches. Like Lughnassadh, Mabon's energy supports decrease. You may want to do spells that set limits, bind enemies, or sever unwanted ties now, too.

Beltane, which takes place when the earth blossoms abundantly with flowering plants and new life, is the ideal day to perform sex magic. In fact, sex has traditionally been a part of this holiday's festivities. Our agrarian ancestors enacted a type of sympathetic magic by making love in the fields to encourage the land's fruitfulness. By spilling their seed on the ground, they symbolically fertilized it. Modern sex magicians still utilize Beltane's fertile energy to nourish their intentions and birth their ideas in the manifest world.

Moon Phases and Magic

The phases of the moon play an important role in magic, too. If your objective involves increase or expansion, perform your ritual or spell during the moon's waxing period (from new to full). This is the time to do spells to attract prosperity, love, success, and so on. As the moon's shape grows, so will your intention.

If you wish to reduce, limit, or let go of something, do magic while the moon is waning (from full to new). As the moon's form diminishes (at least from our vantage point here on earth), so will whatever you've intended. Do magic now to lose weight, cut expenses, or end an unhappy relationship.

The new moon supports new beginnings—the birth of a business or the start of a journey, for instance. The full moon brings pending matters to fruition.

Pay attention to eclipses, too. Solar eclipses, when the moon blocks the sun's light, favor things that involve emotions and intuition: romantic and family relationships, creative pursuits, divination, and spiritual endeavors. Lunar eclipses, when the sun blocks the moon's light, support career issues, public life, and intellectual activities. If you begin something on an eclipse, you'll see developments related to it with subsequent eclipses.

Zodiac Magic

Also take into account the passage of the sun and moon through the signs of the zodiac. The sun remains in each astrological sign for about thirty days, the moon for about two and a half days. When the sun or moon occupies a particular sign, you'll get a helping hand from the cosmos if you do magic that harmonizes with the energies of that sign:

- *Aries:* action, independence, competition, assertiveness, vitality, men

- *Taurus:* money, material possessions, sex, love, fruitfulness

- *Gemini:* communication, intellectual pursuits, short trips, siblings

- *Cancer:* home, family, children, security, nourishment, mother

- *Leo:* leadership, status, recognition, self-expression, creativity

- *Virgo:* work, work relationships, pets, health, service to others

- *Libra:* romantic relationships, business partnerships, social situations, legal matters, the arts, women

- *Scorpio:* power, control, other people's money and resources, investments, hidden knowledge, transformation

- *Sagittarius:* travel, knowledge, higher education, spiritual growth

- *Capricorn:* business, finance, career goals, stability, setting limits, father

- *Aquarius:* friendship, group activities, freedom, change

- *Pisces:* intuition/psychic development, spiritual pursuits, the arts

Your birthday is another high-energy day, and a rite of passage. Each year the cosmos showers you with blessings and opens doors for you on the anniversary of your incarnation in the physical world. This is the time to celebrate and focus on yourself. Do spells and rituals now to support your goals and attract love, prosperity, success, or whatever you desire.

The Future of Sex Magic

Sex magic has been with us always, and I suspect it always will be. During the last few decades the practice has gained popularity in the West, perhaps in reaction to the demystification of sex in modern society. The exploitation of sex by merchandisers, the entertainment industry, and the media, though not unique to this millennium, has become rampant and crass, leaving us with a bad taste in our mouths. The superficial sexual encounters many of us engage in don't satisfy our longing for passion, love, and genuine intimacy; instead they perpetuate our frustration and disillusionment. Although I'd be the last person to advocate a return to the dark ages of sexual repression and Puritanism, somehow the so-called sexual revolution has managed to take the bubbles out of the champagne.

In *Magia Sexualis: Sex, Magic, and Liberation in Modern Western Esotericism,* Hugh B. Urban writes about sex as the "innermost secret or 'hidden truth' of the self, the most powerful force in human nature, and the key to understanding the mysteries of human existence." When was the last time you felt that way during sex?

Through sex magic we become reacquainted with the sacredness and primal power of sex. Suddenly, we find ourselves up close and personal with the "real deal," and it truly does rock our world. Sex magic bridges body and spirit. It awakens the Divine within us and reconnects us with Source, bringing us back to the home we never left and the knowledge we never truly forgot. It lets us see ourselves and our partners as the incredibly amazing beings we are. It awakens us to our unlimited potential, and provides the key to creating the world according to our own designs.

You can have and be anything you choose. At this very moment, you possess the ability to make your life whatever you want it to be—not through working hard and struggling, but through expressing the joy and pleasure that are your birthright.

That's the secret of sex magic. Share it!

resources

Ashton, Dr. Jennifer. "Many Too Tired for Sex, Study Says." *CBS News*, April 20, 2010.

Alexander, Skye. *The Everything Spells & Charms Book.* 2nd Ed. Avon, MA: Adams Media, 2008.

Alexander, Skye. *The Everything Wicca & Witchcraft Book.* 2nd Ed. Avon, MA: Adams Media, 2008.

Alexander, Skye. *The Everything Tarot Book.* 2nd Ed. Avon, MA: Adams Media, 2006.

Alexander, Skye. *Good Spells for Bad Days.* Avon, MA: Adams Media, 2009.

Alexander, Skye. *Magickal Astrology.* Franklin Lakes, NJ: New Page Books/Career Press, 2000.

Alexander, Skye. *Nice Spells/Naughty Spells.* Avon, MA: Adams Media, 2006.

Anand, Margo. *The Art of Sexual Ecstasy: The Path of Sacred Sexuality for Western Lovers.* Los Angeles: Jeremy P. Tarcher, Inc., 1989.

Andrews, Ted. *Animal-Speak: The Spiritual & Magical Powers of Creatures Great & Small.* St. Paul, MN: Llewellyn Publications, 1996.

Anthony, Carol K. *A Guide to the I Ching.* Stow, MA: Anthony Publishing Company, 1982.

Blum, Ralph. *The Book of RuneCards.* New York: Oracle Books/St. Martin's Press, 1989.

Bryner, Jeanna. "For Women, Sex and Happiness Go Hand-in-Hand." *Live Science* (October 5, 2009).

Byrne, Rhonda. *The Secret.* New York: Atria Books, 2006.

Campbell, Don G. *The Mozart Effect.* New York: Harper-Collins Publishers, 2001.

Cooney, Elizabeth. "Trust Me—the Glass is Half Full." *Boston Globe* (March 9, 2009).

Crowley, Aleister. *777 and Other Qabalistic Writings of Aleister Crowley.* York Beach, ME: Samuel Weiser, Inc., 1979.

Crowley, Aleister. *Book 4.* York Beach, ME: Samuel Weiser, Inc., 1980.

Crowley, Aleister. *The Book of Lies.* York Beach, ME: Samuel Weiser, Inc., 1992.

Crowley, Aleister. *The Book of Thoth.* New York: Samuel Weister, Inc., 1974.

Crowley, Aleister, and Lady Freida Harris. *Thoth Tarot.* York Beach, Maine: Samuel Weiser, Inc., 1983, and Stamford, CT: U.S. Games Systems, 1998.

Dethlefsen, Thorwald, and Rudiger Dahlke, M.D. *The Healing Power of Illness*. Shaftesbury, Dorset, England: Element Books, 1990.

Devi, Kamala. *The Eastern Way of Love*. New York: Simon and Schuster, 1977.

Dyer, Wayne W. *The Power of Intention*. Carlsbad, CA: Hay House, 2004.

Emoto, Masaru. *The Hidden Messages in Water*. Hillsboro, OR: Beyond Words Publishing, 2004.

Farrar, Janet and Stewart. *A Witch's Bible*. Blaine, WA: Phoenix Publishing, 1996.

Geller, Joshua. "Basic Techniques of Sex Magick," www.spiritual.com.au.

Goldman, Jonathan. "Greetings & Welcome to the World of Sound Healing." www.healingsounds.com.

Hart, Martin, Ph.D., and Skye Alexander. *The Best Meditations on the Planet*. Beverly, MA: Fair Winds Press, 2011.

Heji, Anja. "Introduction to Sex Magick," www.spiritual.com.au.

Herz, Rachel. *The Scent of Desire*. New York: HarperCollins, 2007.

Hicks, Esther and Jerry. *The Law of Attraction: The Basics of the Teachings of Abraham*. Carlsbad, CA: Hay House, 2006.

Hicks, Esther and Jerry. *Money and the Law of Attraction*. Carlsbad, CA: Hay House, 2008.

Kuchinskas, Susan. "Meditation Heals Body and Mind." *WebMD Magazine* (November 12, 2009).

Knight, Sirona. *Love, Sex, and Magick: Exploring the Spiritual Union Between Male and Female.* Secaucus, NJ: Citadel Press, 1999.

Kraig, Donald Michael. *Modern Sex Magick: Secrets of Erotic Spirituality.* St. Paul, MN: Llewellyn Publications, 1999.

Lady Hecate. "Hecate and Drawing Down the Full Moon," www.hecatescauldron.org.

MacGregor, Trish and Rob. *The 7 Secrets of Synchronicity.* Avon, MA: Adams Media, 2010.

Max, Joseph. "What Is Chaos Magic?" Boudicca's Bard, www.boudicca.de, 1999.

O', Nigris. "An Essay on Sex and Sex Magic." www.spiritual.com.au

Peregrine, Robert A. *Rob's Magick Blog,* http://robjo.wordpress.com.

Randolph, Paschal Beverly. *Eulis! The History of Love.* Toledo, OH: Randolph Publishing Co., 1874.

Reich, Wilhelm. *The Function of the Orgasm.* New York: Bantam, 1967.

Robbins, Tom. *Jitterbug Perfume.* New York: Bantam Dell, 1984.

Schiffer, Nancy. *The Power of Jewelry.* Atglen, PA: Schiffer Publishing, Ltd., 1988.

Simmons, Robert and Naisha Ahsian. *The Book of Stones.* Berkeley: North Atlantic Books, 2007.

Sinetar, Marsha. *Do What You Love and the Money Will Follow: Discovering Your Right Livelihood.* New York: Dell Publishing, 1987.

Sutton, Maya Magee, Ph.D., and Nicholas R. Mann. *Druid Magic.* St. Paul, MN: Llewellyn Publications, 2000.

Teilhard de Chardin, Pierre. *The Phenomenon of Man.* London: William Collins Sons & Co., Ltd. and New York: Harper & Row Publishers, 1959.

Tye, Jeffrey. "Tantra: Sex Magic." www.lycaeum.org/altered/sexmed/sexmagic.htm.

U.D., Frater. *Secrets of Western Sex Magic: Magical Energy and Gnostic Trance.* St. Paul, MN: Llewellyn Publications, 2001.

Urban, Hugh B. *Magia Sexualis: Sex, Magic, and Liberation in Modern Western Esotericism.* Berkeley and Los Angeles: University of California Press, 2006.

Walls, Lori. *Tarot Erotica.* New York: QED Games, Inc.,1999.

Watson, Nancy B. *Practical Solitary Magic.* York Beach, ME: Samuel Weiser, Inc., 1996.

Wilson, Colin. *Aleister Crowley: The Nature of the Beast.* Wellingborough, Northamptonshire: The Aquarian Press, 1987.

Whitcomb, Bill. *The Magician's Companion: A Practical & Encyclopedic Guide to Magical & Religious Symbolism.* St. Paul, MN: Llewellyn Publications, 1998.

index

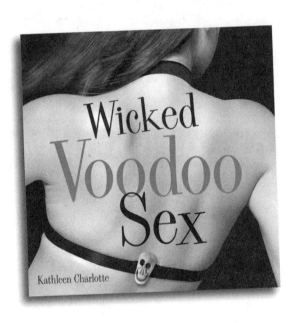

Wicked Voodoo Sex

Kathleen Charlotte

Wicked Voodoo Sex
KATHLEEN CHARLOTTE

Get down and dirty like a Voodoo Goddess!

Kathleen Charlotte invites women to become "spiritual sluts" and embrace the powerful, healing essence of sex—Voodoo style. Provocative and unapologetically candid, this saucy sex guide offers Voodoo-Tantric practices that will invigorate your sex life and enrich your sexual power.

Flirt like a Goddess. Transform your bedroom into a temple of love. Invite Voodoo spirits to take possession during lovemaking. Take a tour of the erogenous zones and discover new ways to stimulate them. By reveling in sex as a holy, healing, and wholesome activity, you'll dispel sexual shame and awaken powerful Goddess energy vital to health and happiness.

Sexual positions, Voodoo trance, astral sex, aphrodisiacs, magic spells, erotic dance, and sexual healing rituals are all covered in this bold and bawdy collection of Voodoo sex secrets.

978-0-7387-1200-0, 264 pp., 7 x 7 $16.95

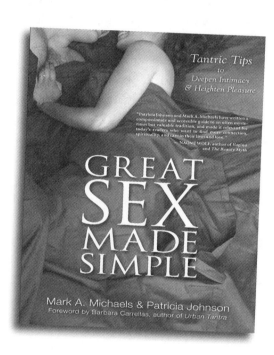

Tantric Tips
to
Deepen Intimacy
& Heighten Pleasure

"Patricia Johnson and Mark A. Michaels have written a compassionate and accessible guide to an often mysterious but valuable tradition, and made it relevant for today's readers who want to find more connection, spirituality, and care in their lives and love."
— NAOMI WOLF, author of *Vagina* and *The Beauty Myth*

GREAT SEX MADE SIMPLE

Mark A. Michaels & Patricia Johnson
Foreword by Barbara Carrellas, author of *Urban Tantra*

Great Sex Made Simple
Tantric Tips to Deepen Intimacy & Heighten Pleasure
Mark A. Michaels and Patricia Johnson

Take your sex life from ordinary to extraordinary with this fun and easy-to-use beginner's guide to authentic Tantra.

Explore new and surprising sources of sensual delight with fifty-four Tantric techniques for enhancing intimacy and deepening pleasure. Proving that Tantric lovemaking doesn't have to take hours, Tantra experts Mark A. Michaels and Patricia Johnson present straightforward, simple practices that anyone can do. Along with fundamental principles of Tantric sex, you will discover amazing ways to prolong arousal, physically and spiritually satisfy your partner, maximize sexual bliss, and reach higher states of consciousness.

978-0-7387-3345-6, 264 pp., 6 x 9 $17.99